WINE-FRIENDLY FOOD SERIES

Companions at Table

Food to Serve
with American-Grown
Italian Varietals

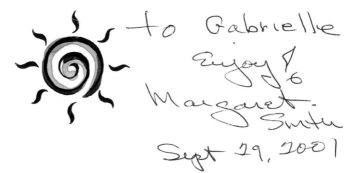

to Gabrielle
Enjoy!
Margaret Smith
Sept 29, 2001

Wine Introduction by Rod Smith

MARGARET ACTON SMITH
BARBARA J. BRAASCH

TOYON HILL PRESS   WOODSIDE, CALIFORNIA

Companions at Table
Food to Serve with American-Grown Italian Varietals
Sangiovese, Barbera, Moscato, Pinot Grigio, Arneis and More

Wine Introduction by Rod Smith
Book Design: Kathy Avanzino Barone
Production: Rex Parcell

Library of Congress Cataloging-in-Publication Data:

Smith, Margaret Acton and Braasch, Barbara J.
Companions at table : food to serve with american-grown italian varietals / by Margaret Acton Smith and Barbara J. Braasch, introduction by Rod Smith
    p. 112
    "Wine-friendly food series"
    Includes index
    ISBN 0-9642901-4-6
1. Cookery. 2. Cookery (wine). 3. Wines.   I. Title.
641.5   98-060470
                                               CIP

Toyon Hill Press
118 Hillside Drive
Woodside, CA 94062-3521
www.toyonhillpress.com

Printed in Canada by Hignell Book Printing   First printing 1998

Contents

· ·

(Continued on page 4)

(…continued from page 3)

Introduction

When you talk to someone who has a passion for wine, you'll soon find that person also has a similar passion for food. It proves an old adage: talk occurs over a meal; conversation takes place over a meal with food and wine. Taking time to sip a glass of wine when you dine is a refreshing experience because people who enjoy both wine and food enhance the dining experience. That is why this book is dedicated to the "pleasure principle" of wine with food.

Many Americans do not yet associate wine with food, yet wine is one of the oldest foods known to humans. *Companions at Table* presents signposts along the way for discovering newly emerging wines to enhance food. Most of the wines are grown on the West Coast of the U.S., mainly in California. Descendants of a long and illustrious Italian lineage, these wines are described by wine writer Rod Smith in his introduction to wine.

Surprisingly, this is not a collection of Italian recipes (although we did include some old favorites), but rather a book that contains foods your neighbors concoct and serve at their table. America is a melting pot of cultures and global produce, so many recipes may have ingredients that may be new to

you. Other recipes are more traditional. We always recommend using the highest quality and freshest ingredients to ensure the greatest pleasure. All recipes have been tested in home kitchens, both for technique and for pleasing matches with Italian American-grown wines.

While it's true that wines and foods from the same region are usually very compatible, we live in new wine-producing territories, and many vines are still young. As they mature and new wines are produced, new food and wine pairings will continue to be made.

In addition to wine and food information, *Companions at Table* contains travel tips for the reader from Barbara Braasch, who will offer ideas for exploring wine-growing regions, make suggestions for the best places to find local wines and foods, and help you discover eateries and food fairs showcasing local cuisine.

We would like to share our information with our readers. For up-to-date information on wines and wineries, food that can be ordered by mail (including Dungeness crab), farmers' markets, food festivals, cooking supplies, recipe credits, and other helpful hints, please use our fax-by-request, page 110.

We hope you enjoy these foods and wines, and perhaps share a glass with a new friend over a meal. That is the purpose of this book. ✿

Margaret Acton Smith

As a travel writer and invitee to more travel forums than I care to remember, I've spent more than 30 years telling people where to go in the western U.S., Alaska, Hawaii, Mexico, Central and South America, Europe, Australia, etc. Usually I was the one with the glass of wine in my hand, sipping frantically as I tried to remember the name of that out-of-the-way hotel that served exotic food that you could actually eat without suffering later! And I'll have to admit, in those days I don't even remember what kind of wine I was drinking or what I was served at the meal!

But times have changed and I've been educated by some of the finest wine growers, winemakers, food and wine writers, and wine judges in the country. My main mentor is Margaret Smith, the co-author of this book and publisher of the Wine-Friendly Food Series. I've been fortunate enough to edit two other wine and food books for Toyon Hill Press and have had the privilege of being part of many food and wine pairings. As Margaret secretly hoped, some of her knowledge was filtered down. I can now proudly announce "I like that" when I'm served the perfect complement of vino and victual.

One of my contributions to this book is to tell you where to find food-related areas, and what else to do while you are there. I'm a fanatic farmers' market fan and food festival buff. If you have never had asparagus ice cream (Stockton) or tried artichoke cookies (Watsonville), I'll show you where to join the fun. To get the maximum winery experience, visit larger wineries during the height of crush, taking tours to view busy activity. Visit the tiny wineries when owners or winemakers have time to explain the virtues of their vinous offerings.

Barbara J. Braasch

Acknowledgments

Many people shared their family recipes. We looked at all very carefully, tested them in our home kitchens, selected the best ideas, and edited them to our specifications. Appreciation and thanks go to the following people for giving *Companions at Table* spice and variety.

Winser Paul Acton; Salem, Oregon
Mug Soup, 30; Baked Beans Plus, 48;
Purely Potatoes, 49; Sweet Beet Salad, 38;
Chicken & Dumplings, 68;
and Pecan Pie, 100

Bill Ardizoia; San Francisco, California
Fire Pit Beef, 78

Kathy Avanzino Barone;
San Carlos, California
Olive Flat Bread, 19

Phil Freese; Healdsburg, California
Fresh Tomato Pasta, 53

John Keller; Lafayette, California
Wild Venison Stew, 93

Luigi Leoni;
Restaurant au Parmesan,
Quebec City, Canada
Linguini Primavera, 55

Paul LeVier; Glendora, California
Roasted Eggplant Soup, 31;
Barbera Stew, 71; Paul's Pot Roast, 84

Joyce Ortega; Hillsborough, California
Cranberry Vinaigrette Salad, 40

Panico Family; Dover Canyon Winery,
Paso Robles, California
Stuffed Beef Fillets (Braciole), 82

Jennifer and Peter Phoenix; Hurst, Texas
Mushroom Risotto, 58; Buffalo Bruschetta, 92

Mick Rosacci; Littleton, Colorado
Sunday Lasagne, 56; Baked Mushroom
Polenta with Asiago Cheese, 60; Peppered
Rib Eye Steak, 80

David Rosenthal; Lafayette, California
Roast Chicken Salad, 36; Sherry-Walnut
Dressing, 36; Summer Eggplant Sandwich, 42;
Couscous with Peppers, Onions & Herbs, 62

Dennis Sienko; Orangevale, California
Smoked Chicken & Bosc Pear Salad, 37; Garlic
Mashed Potatoes, 45; Layered Zucchini &
Potatoes, 46; Tomato Sauce for All Seasons, 50;
Parsley-Garlic Chicken, 66; Honey Tangerine
and Moscato Sauce, 96

Sarah J. Walker; Santa Rosa, California
Grilled Beef with Wine Marinade, 79

Chef Tim Fisher; Portola Café,
Monterey Bay Aquarium, California
Chipolte Dressing, 41

A Note on New World Italian Wines

Nearly two thousand years ago, the Roman writer Pliny the Elder noted in his *Naturalis Historae* that there were 91 separate wine grape varieties being cultivated in the Roman Empire. The best of those, in his opinion, were a scant dozen cultivated in the heart of Italy, and he claimed that they were indigenous. Among them, he said, were the vines that had yielded the famous Falernian wine of 121 BC, when Opimius was Consul—a legendary vintage already as distant from Pliny then as Bordeaux's great "Comet Vintage" of 1811 is from us.

What varieties those vines were in modern terms is hard to tell. The recent discovery of ancient grape seeds from an excavation at Pompeii, which was destroyed by an eruption of Mt. Vesuvius in the year of Pliny's death (79 AD), has given some insight; DNA sampling indicates that the wine people were drinking in ancient Pompeii was made from some of the same grapes that are found in the Campania region today. Interestingly, viticulture in Campania has seriously declined during the last century, and those grape seeds from the past have given it new life—but one founded on an ancient and noble history, as if modern Italians could find in a glass of Aglianico the actual aromas and flavors of the Falernian wines drunk by their distant ancestors.

So might we, here in the 20th century New World, find echoes of ancient Rome and modern Italy in a glass of Aglianico wine from, say,

Amador County in California's Sierra Nevada foothills. The soil and climate are different, of course. So is the cultivation of the vines and the winemaking procedures. In fact, everything is different—except the grape. It's as if Bacchus himself had delivered the stuff of Falernian wine to California, just as he is said to have brought it to Italy in some distant

mythological time. And who knows? Maybe he did.

At this point Aglianico plantings in the United States can be counted in vines rather than acres, yet it gains ground steadily each year, as do more substantial plantings of other grapes whose names roll off the American tongue with the promise of sensual mysteries: *Sangiovese, Nebbiolo, Pinot Grigio, Refosco, Barbera, Moscato, Arneis…*

These are all grapes that have been cultivated in Italy for a very long time, long enough to become so closely attuned with their regional soils and climates that they consistently yield superb wines with unique aromas and flavors. In the last few years they have become the rising stars of New World wine, particularly in California, Washington, Oregon, and several other American states.

This book provides recipes developed especially to go with these neo-Italian wines. More than that—and this is the wine lover's voice momentarily shouting over that of the cook—it offers a way to explore the many sensual facets of some of the world's most wonderful wines.

To me the difference between the Old and New World renditions of these grapes is basically one of scale and intensity, reflecting distinct natural and cultural aesthetics: the vibrant subtlety of Caravaggio or Tintoretto compared with the vivid classical realism of Richard Piccolo, whose epic paintings comprising the "Allegory of the Elements" in Sacramento (U.S. Bank Plaza, 1990-'93) show a strong Italian Renaissance influence and yet

are so intensely American in their treatment of color and light. Or the difference between the bold Californian paintings of Richard Diebenkorn, with his wide-open color planes and Californian palette, and one of the more elegant and subtle Italian masters—Leonardo, let's say, who set his famous portrait of Mona Lisa Gherardini in a soft Tuscan landscape.

The neo-Italian varietal movement is fundamentally similar to the Rhône revival, but there are important differences. One is that while the Rhône grapes come from a single region with closely defined soils and climate, the Italians have more diverse origins. The areas within Italy that produce Sangiovese, Nebbiolo, Pinot Grigio, and the seemingly countless other grapes grown throughout the noble boot-shaped peninsula are quite diverse in their soils and climates, not to mention long-standing methods of vinification.

Another difference is that Italian wine is currently in evolutionary overdrive, which means that the Italian models that are being emulated here are moving targets. To take just one example, American Sangiovese producers look to the grape's ancient home, the Chianti region in Tuscany, for inspiration—yet the Chianti producers have undertaken an unprecedented self-reinvention of viticulture and winemaking in the nineties. So the Americans are on their own—and they're taking that seriously.

The Consorzio Cal-Italia, a coalition of California producers formed in 1997, is a large, focused, and well-supported organization. There are currently more than a hundred California wineries producing Italian varietals and varietal blends, another dozen or so in Washington and other states. Their wines vary widely in aromas and flavors, but all can be said to have one virtue that the old standby varietals, Chardonnay and Cabernet Sauvignon, can't always claim: they're terrific with food.

Red Wines
· · · · · · · · · · · · · · · · · ·

🍇 **Sangiovese**, the primary red grape of Chianti, is all the rage at the moment. The name is probably a corruption of the Latin term *sanguis Jovis*, meaning "Jove's blood." That's appropriate. Jove, or Jupiter, was one of the most brilliant gods of ancient Mediterranean culture, and initiates of Sangiovese do indeed find divinity in the regal red wine of his namesake grape. Sangiovese wine is not particularly

bloodlike in color or thickness—not like Nebbiolo, Tempranillo, Syrah, Cabernet Sauvignon, or the many deep red Mediterranean grapes—but its vibrant intensity may indeed be called sanguine. Furthermore, it shares with other great wine grapes a godlike capacity to surprise and dazzle the senses.

Sangiovese is a wily animal from the sensory standpoint. Like all the world's most valued wine grapes (particularly Pinot Noir and Cabernet Sauvignon, both of which it resembles in certain ways), it is particularly sensitive to its surroundings; thus wine from a well-located vineyard can reflect soil and climate and vintage to an uncommon degree. And like its noble peers, it resists absolute categorization. Sangiovese comes in many subtle forms: there is great Sangiovese, yet there is no such thing as definitive Sangiovese. It typically has a lot of fruity flavor without being dense or rich. The intensity of Sangiovese's fruit flavor belies its delicacy, which is a challenge to winemakers. Aging it in small oak barrels, a relatively recent practice influenced by French-cum-Californian winemaking, can deaden the fruit if not done with restraint. A big Sangiovese can be tannic enough to bear a resemblance to young Bordeaux, but even then there is an underlying softness which is seldom found in claret, along with a seductive exuberance that seems particularly Italian.

The oldest known Sangiovese vineyard in California is on the Seghesio Winery estate in northern Sonoma County. Approaching ninety years old, those vines have provided budwood for new plantings throughout the state. Many growers have also obtained budwood for propagation from Atlas Peak Vineyards, planted high above the Napa Valley by the Antinori family who brought selected clones from their long-established vineyards in Tuscany.

Barbera comes second in excitement, although there are far more acres of Barbera than Sangiovese in the U.S. It arrived with Italian immigrants in the 19th century and became the jug-red standby for generations, in large part because its naturally high acidity stood up well to the blazing sun in the San Joaquin Valley. Barbera also loves coastal California's volcanic soils, but perhaps it does even better in the weathered granitic soils of the Sierra Nevada foothills, where it was extensively planted by wise Italian gold-miners-turned-homesteaders, who knew good Barbera ground when they saw it (Zinfandel and Carignane ground too, for that matter). The problem with Barbera has been to tame the naturally high acidity and balance it with concentrated flavor.

Nebbiolo, the red grape of Barolo and Barbaresco, shows great promise in California. A fine Nebbiolo has the quality of an Italian Renaissance painting: the colors and textures are otherworldly, and yet the eyes of the subject follow you intently wherever you stand in the room. Call it a kind of sensory presence.

The very name of the grape suggests an affinity with coastal California. In the high country of Italy's Piedmonte district a creamy fog often rolls out of the Alps to drape the vineyards and shield the burgeoning grapes from heat. They call the fog *il nebi*. Perhaps not coincidentally, the nebi and its effects on wine are mirrored by the cool marine fogs that roll into California's coastal grape-growing areas throughout the growing season, tempering summer heat so that the grapes ripen slowly and evenly. Nebbiolo's characteristic tannin makes it a good candidate for rosato in California.

Refosco is another promising red grape that sells itself to wine lovers easily, sip by sip. Could Refosco be the perfect pizza wine? It may be silly to think that just one of Italy's many wonderful regional wines could bear such an exalted crown (one of my college roommates, a theology student, often asserted that the manna God sent from heaven was, in fact, a kind of pizza). On the other hand, once having slurped a tasty young Refosco with the kind of crusty, savory, full-flavored pizza one finds in Italy, it's hard to imagine any wine complementing it better. California Refosco is quite different from what one drinks from pitchers in Friuli trattorias, but then, California pizza is different, too. Both are bigger, richer, larger in scale and sensory impact. And the match is just as good. To date only a few growers and winemakers have undertaken the Refosco challenge, but it's likely that as more people try it (especially with pizza) the more demand there will be for this lip-smacking, delightfully edgy mouthful of juicy grapes.

OTHER RED VARIETALS

We've already looked at **Aglianico** as emblematic of the historical throughline represented by Italian varietals in the U.S. However, there is very little Aglianico wine being made here at this time, and quality is so far uneven. The density of ripe flavor and tannin of this grape presents a challenge to growers and winemakers. The best Italian Aglianicos have a laser-fine focus on the palate that tethers all the chewy richness and complexity the grape has to offer; so far I haven't tasted any American Aglianicos that quite manage such a deft balancing act, but I have tasted some delicious ones with clear potential. And then, there's **Charbono**, a rare and excellent red Italian variety (possibly the same as Dolcetto) that's been grown and vinified in California as long as Zinfandel and Petite Sirah. Don't bet on a big Charbono revival, but keep a weather eye out for the gradual appearance of more tasty Charbonos, from dedicated small producers as well as from large ones that butter their bread with generic Chardonnay and Merlot.

A final note on reds: the **blends** are coming. Now that American producers are well underway in the process of figuring out where to grow the Italian grapes and how to make them into good wines, there is sure to be increasing experimentation with affinities that may result in some appealing blends. One such affinity, between Sangiovese and Cabernet Sauvgnion, is already well-established. It first appeared in Chianti with the so-called Super Tuscan wines introduced by Antinori in the 1980s. The Super Tuscan idea has caught on big in California, especially in the Napa Valley.

Stay tuned for a trend toward proprietary blends of other Italian grapes in the next few years, and keep "Companions at Table" handy for recipes to go with them.

WHITE WINES
· · · · · · · · · · · · · · · · · · · ·

Thank goodness, not all Italian wine grapes are red. Some of the best grapes Italy has sent us yield lovely white wines, and Margaret and Barbara offer marvelous recipes to go with them—Fish in Ginger-Wine Sauce, for example, is perfection with a nicely chilled Pinot Grigio.

Pinot Grigio is a delight. Don't look for strong sensations here. The point of Pinot Grigio is to complement food flavors and keep the palate fresh throughout a meal, which is why it's one of the most widely planted white wine grapes, not only in Italy but all over the world.

The ideal Pinot Grigio is just slightly heavier than air, pale but brilliant, its delicate perfume wafting from the glass with hints of clean, wet stone and wildflowers, caressing the palate with a lilting acidity. A fine Pinot Grigio gives me the feeling of walking in an alpine meadow just after a spring rain. Our West Coast versions are riper, naturally, and thus more assertive than the Italian model. Still, American Pinot Grigio is the lightest, freshest wine we have in these days of syrupy Chardonnays and heavy, barrel-fermented Sauvignon Blancs. Are you looking for a bright, refreshing white wine to add a little something to lunch without taking over the table? Choose Pinot Grigio. In fact, don't just choose it, keep a bottle or two in the refrigerator at all times.

One note to head off potential confusion: wine consumers facing a shelf of wine labels may notice California and Washington wines called Pinot Grigio side by side with Oregon wines called Pinot Gris. The grape is the same, but the style of wine is different. Alsace producers tend to honor the grape's close relationship to Pinot Noir by rendering Pinot Gris as a richer, fuller-bodied, more serious wine than the Italian Pinot Grigio, and Oregon producers (most of whom obtained their plant material from Alsace rather than Italy) have generally adopted that model as a stylistic counterpart to their famous Pinot Noir. For a lighthearted, fresh, quaffable wine, stick with Pinot Grigio.

🍷 If Pinot Grigio is pure delight, then **Moscato** is glowing optimism. Open a bottle of Moscato on a cold, rainy day and you're instantly reminded that it's sunny and warm somewhere in the world.

Sip Moscato on a searing afternoon and be instantly refreshed. That's what kind of grape Moscato is—somehow it emphasizes the simple pleasure of being alive.

That's not to say, however, that Moscato is a great table wine. In fact, most people find that its assertive aroma and super-fruity palate are at odds with most foods. Moscato is best as a late afternoon wine, with a bowl of salted nuts and perhaps a tangy goat cheese close at hand, and the mesquite burning down to coals in the grill. In fact, the scent of mesquite charcoal in the twilight summer air is a divine accompaniment to Moscato, and the only one it really needs to inspire a heightened sensuality, preparing palate and soul for that sublime

moment when the lamb comes off the grill and the Sangiovese is poured.

And what is Moscato? You had to ask. The short answer is that Moscato is Muscat; the long answer requires a lot of books, maps, and heated discussion. Muscat is a confusing category of wine grape. There are many variations, but the Moscato most planted in Italy is Moscato Bianco, sometimes called Moscato di Canelli, and most Moscato wines made in the U.S. are also White Muscat or Muscat Canelli. All one really needs to know is that a good Moscato wine delivers an impression of sweetness even when made in a dry style—it just can't help itself.

Arneis remains well this side of critical mass as a varietal wine, but a few early releases have the cognoscenti excited. In Italy's Piedmonte this white grape has historically been used as a blending component to lighten up dark, tannic Nebbiolo wines, as Viognier and Roussanne are used to soften heavy Grenache and Syrah in the southern Rhône. On its own, Arneis offers attractions that are similar to Roussanne's: an evocative perfume of exotic blooms and sweet nuts, particularly almonds, and a sensual texture in the mouth. The challenge to growers is finding locations that are warm enough to develop the grape's lovely perfume and flavors, yet cool enough to preserve its tenuous acidity; winemakers have to realize that despite its assertiveness, Arneis is by nature rather delicate, which rules out excessive oak. When everything falls into place, Arneis wines have the flavor and fine, dry palate to succeed where an overblown Chardonnay fails, especially with flavorful seafood such as salmon and prawns.

The intense California sun yields an added bonus with these Italian grape varieties: yummy pink wines. The certainty of ripeness makes it possible to produce excellent **rosatos** from Sangiovese, Nebbiolo, Aglianico, and other red grapes. Such wines can come from opposite sides of the winemaking process. Most are purposefully made rosatos, free-run juice taken off the skins. Others are byproducts of red wines, the result of bleeding juice out of tanks to further concentrate color and flavor in the reds. That type of rosato tends to be stiffer and more tannic, more like light red wines than tinted whites. Either way, a dry and fragrant rosato has a way of heightening simple pleasure.

An Amador County Nebbiolo rosato, for example, glows in the glass like sunset on the pink granite cliffs of the Sierra, while its gently spicy fragrance is the very scent of dusk. That luminous wine and the fragrance of the grill add up to heaven in California.

Despite all this activity, it's unlikely that we'll ever see American wines made from most of Italy's really distinctive grapes. There are hundreds of them; each would require years of dedicated effort to find the right location and winemaking adjustments. They are usually associated with individual villages, and the villages are mostly small and remote, which is why the grapes and their wines have developed so differently in each vicinity that regional varieties like Vien and Vernaccia are usually named for the village, *i.e.* Vien de Nus, or Vernaccia de San Gimigniano. There is a whole category of grapes under the heading Petit Rouge—the "small red" grape, its wines carrying local names. Perhaps, in a thousand years or so, we will have such grapes in California— Sangiovese di Forestville, for example, or Barbera d'Angel's Camp, or Nebbiolo della Mission Santa Maria. The village grapes of Italy, however, will remain in Italy, an eternal encouragement to travel.

As for the ones that are here now, I can't help wondering, how might the hierarchy of grape varieties translate from Italy to America? Like human immigrants, the vines have been given new opportunities to excel and show hidden qualities here in the New World. Sangiovese is everyone's darling today, but might it someday be eclipsed by Aglianico, or

Refosco, or some blend of grapes we haven't encountered yet? Don't be surprised if we're all surprised by how it turns out. Pliny the Elder and his contemporaries were still talking about the Falernian wine of 121 BC two hundred years after the vintage. What sensual marvels await us here in the New World, now that some of those noble and ancient grapes are among us?

That's something to ponder over Buffalo Bruschetta and a glass of Sangiovese. In that combination, and the others in this book, the past meets the future—and the future is ours for the tasting.

Rod Smith
San Francisco

Biography

Rod Smith is writer-at-large for *Wine & Spirits* magazine, where his essays have chronicled the unfolding history of the modern wine culture since 1981. In recent *Wine and Spirits* essays he has written about Portugal's ancient grape varieties and "New Wave" Australian Rieslings. A 1996 essay, "Power, Finesse, and the Well-Made Chardonnay" was nominated for a James Beard Foundation award.

Rod also contributes articles on wine, travel, and sailing—combining all three as often as possible—to a variety of other publications. Subjects of recent magazine articles include flying around Africa in a small plane and sailing among Scotland's famous island distilleries (*Polo*), sailing in the wake of 18th century explorer Matthew Flinders off the Australian coast (*Private Clubs*), and the re-emergence of Chile's long wine tradition (*Appellation*). For several years he wrote a weekly wine column for the *San Francisco Chronicle*.

Rod contributed an afterword to the fine press edition of J. M. Scott's classic novella, *The Man Who Made Wine* (Yolla Bolly Press, 1996), and has also written an introduction to *Rhône Appétit* cookbook published in 1998 by Toyon Hill Press. He wrote the revised edition of *Wine Country: California* (Sunset Books, 1987).

Rod is a fourth-generation Oregonian. He has lived in San Francisco for 22 years with his wife and several small predators.

APPETIZERS

From Asian Roasted Mushrooms to Herbed Turkey Meatballs, this intriguing new collection of hors d'oeuvres contains a sampling of cuisine from around the world. We focus on fresh ingredients, encouraging you to visit farmers' markets and grow your own herbs. And we keep the busy cook in mind: most appetizers are easy to assemble or may be prepared in advance.

Quick Herb Sticks

IT'S HANDY TO KEEP PUFF PASTRY IN YOUR FREEZER

FOR APPETIZERS ON DEMAND. THIS RECIPE IS A GOOD MATCH FOR EITHER

PINOT GRIGIO OR SANGIOVESE WINE.

1 package (17¼ ounces) frozen puff pastry, thawed

1 tablespoon anise **or** fennel seed, crushed

1 egg white, lightly beaten with 1 teaspoon water

Unfold pastry sheets and cut each into eighths. Then cut each piece into 2 triangles. Sprinkle evenly with crushed seeds.

Starting with the longest side, roll each triangle into a stick. Place each stick, center point down, 1 inch apart on a 12- by 15-inch baking sheet. Brush lightly with egg white.

Preheat oven to 400°. Bake sticks until golden brown, about 15 minutes. If made ahead, let cool, wrap until airtight, and refrigerate up to 5 days. Reheat before serving.

Makes 32 appetizers

It's easy to reheat puff pastry sticks or other baked goods in a preheated oven.

Preheat oven to 450°. Lay bread sticks on a cookie sheet and place in oven. Turn oven off. Remove sticks after 5 minutes.

Wrap bread or rolls in aluminum foil and place in hot oven. Turn oven off. Remove bread after 15 minutes. Bread or rolls may remain in oven as long as 45 minutes.

Olive Flat Bread

SERVE HOT OUT OF THE OVEN OR LET MELLOW FOR A DAY.
EITHER WAY IT IS DELICIOUS. USE DIFFERENT KINDS OF OLIVES SUCH AS
BLACK, GREEN OR KALAMATA TO MAKE VARIATIONS WITH THIS BREAD.

2 cans **or** jars pitted olives (about 6 ounces **each**)

5 cups bread **or** all-purpose flour

1 teaspoon salt

2 packages quick-rising yeast

1 teaspoon sugar

1½ cups warm water

½ cup olive oil

1 teaspoon leaf thyme

2 tablespoons oregano

Sea salt **or** kosher salt, for garnish

> *To vary Olive Flat Bread, use different kinds of pitted olives such as black, green, or Kalamata. Pimiento-stuffed olives give a holiday touch to the bread.*

Coarsely chop two-thirds of the olives, reserving one-third for garnish.

Put 4 cups of flour and salt in a food processor. Dissolve yeast and sugar in water before adding to flour. Add olive oil. Process for 20 seconds.

Spread remaining flour on bread board or counter top. Place dough on the floured surface. Knead for a few minutes, until soft and elastic. Knead in chopped olives and thyme. Place dough in a bowl to rise until double in bulk, 45 minutes to 1 hour.

Punch down dough, then knead for 1 or 2 minutes. Roll out dough on a floured board with a floured rolling pin to a thickness of about ½-inch. Place on an oiled baking sheet, spreading the dough with your hands.

Sprinkle with oregano and salt and garnish with reserved whole olives. Let rise 30 minutes.

Preheat oven to 400°. Just before placing dough in the oven, make depressions all over the dough with a wooden spoon handle. Bake 25 minutes. Remove from oven, brush top with olive oil, and sprinkle again with salt.

Cut into 2-inch strips to serve.

Makes 30 to 35 pieces

Caramelized Onion & Pepper Dip

THIS COLORFUL RED DIP IS PERFECT FOR SLICED FRESH VEGETABLES, SUCH AS
JICAMA, KOHLRABI, TURNIPS, CELERY, AND LETTUCE SPEARS.

2 tablespoons olive oil

3 large onions, thinly sliced

2 jars (7¼ ounces **each**) roasted red peppers

2 teaspoons fresh thyme leaves **or** 1 teaspoon dry thyme

2 tablespoons tomato paste

½ cup dry Monterey Jack **or** Parmesan cheese, grated

½ cup ricotta cheese

Heat oil in a large sauté or frying pan. Add onions and cook, stirring occasionally, over medium heat until onions are golden and very soft, about 30 minutes. Add red peppers, thyme, and tomato paste and cook, stirring until heated through and bubbly, about 3 minutes. Let cool.

Place mixture in a food processor or blender. Add cheeses and whirl until puréed. At this point, dip may be covered and refrigerated up to 2 days. Bring to room temperature before serving.

Makes 4 cups

Fresh Herb & Cheese Dip

THIS TASTY, EASY-TO-PREPARE DIP GOES WELL WITH THE BOUNTY
OF SUMMER VEGETABLES—GREEN BEANS, SLICED SUMMER SQUASH,
AND CHERRY TOMATOES.

1 cup sour cream

1 small package (3 ounces) cream cheese

¼ cup crumbled feta cheese

1 tablespoon **each** chopped fresh sage, basil, and thyme **or** 1 teaspoon each dry herbs

1 clove garlic, minced **or** pressed

⅓ cup (3 ounces) crumbled blue cheese

Mix together sour cream, cream cheese, feta cheese, herbs, and garlic until smooth. Stir in blue cheese.

Cover and refrigerate at least 2 hours or up to 3 days.

Makes 1½ cups

Cheese Fondue

SERVE THIS SIMPLE FONDUE WARM OR AT ROOM TEMPERATURE
WITH A BOTTLE OF SANGIOVESE, BARBERA, OR ANY OF THE
NEW AMERICAN-GROWN ITALIAN VARIETALS.

2 packages (8 ounces **each**) cream cheese

½ cup milk

1 cup (5 ounces) freshly grated Parmigiano-Reggiano **or** Parmesan cheese

1 clove garlic, pressed **or** minced (optional)

1 baguette

Sliced fresh vegetables (optional)

Place cream cheese, milk, cheese, and garlic in a double boiler or pan set over hot water. Bring water to a simmer and heat cheese mixture. Stir to combine ingredients.

Slice baguette into ¼-inch rounds. Cut vegetables into shapes for dipping.

Warm a ceramic dish and fill halfway with fondue. Leave space for dipping without dripping. Place dish on a large platter and surround with bread and vegetables.

Makes 2 cups

Asian Roasted Mushrooms

PEANUT BUTTER, HONEY, AND SOY SAUCE?

IT IS THE COMBINATION OF THESE INGREDIENTS—AND OTHERS—THAT IMPARTS

THE PACIFIC RIM FLAVOR TO THIS SPECIAL MUSHROOM DISH.

YOU NEED TO START YOUR PREPARATIONS AT LEAST A DAY IN ADVANCE.

1 tablespoon creamy peanut butter

¼ cup Pinot Grigio wine **or** sake

1 teaspoon grated fresh ginger

2 teaspoons honey

2 tablespoons lemon juice

2 tablespoons rice vinegar **or** wine vinegar

1 tablespoon soy sauce

1 pound (approximately 16) brown, white, **or** shiitake mushrooms

Mix together peanut butter, wine, ginger, honey, lemon juice, vinegar, and soy sauce until blended. Add mushrooms and stir to coat. Place in a zip-lock plastic bag or a non-corrosive bowl and refrigerate overnight or up to 2 days.

Preheat oven to 450°. Line a rimmed cookie sheet with aluminum foil. Place mushrooms, cap side down, on sheet. Drizzle with marinade. Bake for 10 minutes.

Remove from oven, turn mushrooms over, baste with marinade, and return to oven. Bake 5 minutes more.

Serve mushrooms hot or at room temperature.

Makes 16 appetizers

Travel Tip

To get into a Pacific Rim frame of mind, visit San Francisco's Chinatown, home to more Chinese than any other place in the world outside China.

Several walking tours feature a culinary look at this 16-square-block area. For more information, turn to the Resource Guide, page 110.

Eggplant Rollups

THIS SUMMER STARTER IS A GOOD CHOICE TO PAIR

WITH WHITE ITALIAN WINES GROWN IN THE U.S.A.

1 pound (about 4) Italian **or** Asian eggplants

2 tablespoons olive oil

4 ounces fresh goat cheese, plain **or** herb-crusted

1 bunch watercress **or** parsley

Like its tomato and pepper cousins, eggplant is an annual fruit commonly called a vegetable. The large, oval, purple variety is most familiar, though yellow, green, and white varieties are available.

Preheat the oven to 450°. Cut eggplant lengthwise into ¼-inch slices. Brush both sides with olive oil. Place a single layer on a non-stick or foil-lined baking sheet and bake 8 minutes. Turn eggplant over and bake another 5 minutes or until very soft when pressed. Let cool.

Place a teaspoon of cheese at an end of each eggplant slice, then roll it up. If the roll becomes too large, cut eggplant in half crosswise. Secure with a round toothpick. At this point, the eggplant may be covered and refrigerated up to 1 day.

Bring the roll ups to room temperature before serving.

To serve, place rollups on a platter, topping each one with a watercress sprig.

Makes 12 to 16 appetizers

Herbed Turkey Meatballs

SAGE AND FENNEL GO WELL WITH BOTH PINOT GRIGIO AND SANGIOVESE.
MAKE MEATBALLS IN ADVANCE, REFRIGERATE, AND REHEAT TO ROOM
TEMPERATURE IN A MICROWAVE OR, COVERED, IN THE OVEN.

1 pound ground turkey **or** other
ground meat

¼ cup minced fresh sage leaves **or**
1 teaspoon dry sage

1 teaspoon crushed fennel seeds

¼ teaspoon **each** salt and fresh ground
pepper

Mustard (optional) for dipping

Thoroughly mix all ingredients except mustard. Shape mixture into 1-inch balls.

Preheat oven to 450°. Line a baking sheet with aluminum foil. Place meatballs on baking sheet about 1 inch apart. Bake, turning once, until meat is no longer pink in the center, about 8 minutes.

Serve at room temperature with your favorite mustard.

Makes 24 meatballs

> Keep your spices and herbs fresh by storing them in a cool dark place. When the good aromas are gone, it is time to get a new supply. Whole spices keep longer than ground or leaf herbs. Pick herbs from your garden or buy fresh herbs from your local produce market.

Thai Beef on Lettuce Spears

FRESH FLAVORS—WITH A BIT OF SPICE—MAKE THIS APPETIZER SPECIAL.
CRISP LETTUCE ADDS JUST THE RIGHT CRUNCH.

¼ cup short **or** long-grain rice

2 heads romaine lettuce

1 pound lean ground beef

1 teaspoon sugar

½ teaspoon crushed red pepper

½ cup **each** thinly sliced green onions and chopped cilantro

2 tablespoons chopped fresh mint

¼ cup lemon juice

1½ tablespoons soy sauce **or** fish sauce

Heat a large frying or sauté pan to medium hot. Add rice and cook, stirring, until golden, about 5 minutes. Remove from heat and cool. Place rice in a food processor or blender and whirl until finely ground. Set aside.

Wash lettuce, discard outer leaves, separate spears, and cut into 3-inch-long pieces for dipping. Over high heat, crumble and cook beef, stirring, until no longer pink. Remove any excess fat. Stir in rice, sugar, red pepper, onions, cilantro, mint, lemon juice, and soy sauce. Heat through and cook for about 1 minute.

Transfer mixture into a serving bowl and surround with lettuce spears. Guests use lettuce spears to dip into the meat. Have plenty of napkins on hand. Thai Beef can be made ahead and reheated in a microwave.

Makes 30 appetizers

Ham with Pears

THIS QUICK-TO-FIX APPETIZER GOES WELL WITH EITHER WHITE OR RED WINE.
YOU'LL PROBABLY HAVE MOST OF THE STAPLES, INCLUDING WOODEN
TOOTHPICKS, ON YOUR PANTRY SHELVES.

5 ounces thinly sliced cooked ham

3 medium size, firm-ripe pears, washed but not peeled

¼ cup catsup

1 teaspoon dry mustard

1 tablespoon brown sugar

2 tablespoons soy sauce

1 small clove garlic, minced **or** pressed

Cut ham into 1-inch-wide strips. Core pears and cut each pear into 8 wedges. Then cut each wedge in half. Wrap a strip of ham around each piece and secure with a toothpick.

In a small bowl, mix together catsup, mustard, brown sugar, soy sauce, and garlic.

Arrange pears in a flat microwave dish and spoon sauce over each piece. Heat in a microwave oven until ham is sizzling and pears are heated through (about 30 seconds). Place remaining sauce in a bowl for dipping. Set bowl on a large plate and surround with pears. Serve warm.

Makes 48 appetizers

> At farmers' markets, roadside stands, and specialty produce stores, you'll usually be offered samples of the fruits and vegetables for sale. It's a good way to test the ripeness and flavor of fruits like pears.

Instant Appetizers

SOMETIMES YOU JUST DON'T HAVE TIME TO PREPARE APPETIZERS.
WHEN UNEXPECTED COMPANY DROPS BY, TRY ONE OF THESE TASTY TREATS.
ALL PAIR WELL WITH PINOT GRIGIO, SANGIOVESE, AND BARBERA.

*Prepare an attractive assortment of cheeses, such as Cheddar (Tillamook **or** English), Swiss (Jarlsberg **or** Emmenthaler), hard cheese (Dry jack **or** Parmesan), Blue cheese (Oregon blue **or** Gorgonzola), fresh **or** aged Goat cheese, and Brie.*

Have your guests sample different varieties and pick their favorites to go with the wine you serve.

Asiago Cheese, Olive Oil & Crusty Bread

Grate cheese into a dipping bowl, place slices of crusty bread in a basket, and pour extra virgin olive oil onto a butter plate. Have guests dip pieces of bread in oil and then dip them into the cheese.

Smoked Salmon & Fresh Goat Cheese on Baguettes

Buy a 1-inch-thick piece of western smoked salmon (not lox). Place salmon on a platter with two forks (for flaking off the meat) and a 5-ounce round of fresh goat cheese. Provide a knife for spreading the cheese and a basket of bread. If you don't have bread, rye crackers make a good substitute. Place cheese on bread, top with salmon, and enjoy with a bottle of Pinot Grigio.

Pocket Bread, Yoghurt & Sprouts

Cut each pocket bread into 6 triangles. Do not separate top from bottom. Spoon plain yoghurt into each triangle and top with alfalfa or radish sprouts.

Small Plates

MANY OF THE MOST POPULAR NEW RESTAURANTS ARE OFFERING
A SELECTION OF SMALL PLATES ON THEIR MENUS.
DINERS MAY SELECT SEVERAL SMALL PLATES AS APPETIZERS TO
ACCOMPANY WINE OR AS SUBSTITUTES FOR SINGLE ENTRÉES.

For company or large family meals, you may want to serve something at the table for guests to nibble on until last-minute preparations are complete. Prepare enough appetizer plates to serve four people each and let guests help themselves.

As a general rule, each plate should contain crisp, soft, fresh, and savory combinations.

SAMPLER PLATE
(4 pieces each):

Asian Roasted Mushrooms (page 22) on a bed of shredded radishes

Pork Tenderloin (page 88), thinly sliced

Marinated Fresh Vegetables

Canelli Bean Salad (page 39)

Olive Flat Bread (page 19)

Asiago **or** Dry jack cheese, thinly sliced

OTHER CANDIDATES:

Baked Mushroom Polenta (page 60)

Baked Beans Plus (page 48)

Eggplant Rollups (page 23)

Cheeses, meats, salads, **or** olives

Each plate serves 4

SOUPS, SALADS & SIDES

The titles of our innovative recipes for starter courses or side dishes reveal their ingredient variety, seasonal nature, and global context: Spring Vegetable Soup, Sweet Beet Salad, Pacific Rim Chicken Broth, and Baby Bok Choy. You'll discover new ways with fresh greens and vegetables and new twists on old favorites: Garlic Mashed Potatoes and Baked Beans Plus.

Whether you are a vegetarian or just interested in a healthy diet, this may be the chapter to which you turn most often.

Mug Soup

A GREAT HOT FIRST COURSE TO SERVE WHILE GUESTS ARE GATHERING.

3 large leeks

2 medium russet potatoes

2 cups water

½ teaspoon salt

1 tablespoon parsley, finely chopped

½ cup Pinot Grigio **or** other white wine

Wash leeks thoroughly, removing all sand, and slice the white and tender green parts into ½-inch rounds. Peel potatoes and dice to match leeks.

Place leeks, potatoes, and salt into a stock pot; add water. Bring to a boil, turn heat down, and simmer for 40 minutes. Add parsley and remove from heat.

Using a food mill, blender, or food processor, purée soup. Return soup to pot and add wine, whisking to mix. Thin to desired consistency with water, wine, or cream. Keep warm or reheat in a double boiler.

Pour into mugs and serve warm or cold.

Serves 4 to 6

Mug Soup is also delicious served cold on a warm summer day. For rich flavor, substitute non-dairy creamer, milk, or cream for wine. Pinot Grigio or Arneis are good wine choices.

You may want to add other vegetables to your potato-leek soup for color and flavor variety. When you add vegetables, add another ½-cup water during cooking.

Experiment with your favorite vegetables. Some suggestions are listed below:

1 cup diced sweet potatoes *or* **squash** plus **½-teaspoon ground cloves**	**1 cup baby carrots** *plus* **1 teaspoon ground ginger** *or* **minced fresh ginger**
1 cup broccoli buds (to keep color, add to broth in the last 5 minutes of cooking)	**1 cup diced seeded cucumbers** *plus* **1 teaspoon dill weed**

Roasted Eggplant Soup

A REFRESHING VEGETABLE SOUP TO SERVE AS A FIRST COURSE
WITH A CRUSTY BREAD. ITALIAN VARIETAL WINE CHOICES
INCLUDE TOCAI FRIULANO AND BARBERA.

1 large eggplant, 1½ pounds

3 medium tomatoes

1 small onion

1 head garlic

2 tablespoons olive oil

6 cups vegetable **or** chicken broth

1 teaspoon leaf thyme

1 cup half and half

Feta cheese for garnish

Cut eggplant in half lengthwise; cut tomatoes and onion in half crosswise. Cut ¼-inch off top of garlic head. Place vegetables on foil-lined baking pan. Brush lightly with olive oil. Bake in a 400° oven for 45 minutes. Don't worry if some browned or burned spots appear. Let vegetables cool.

Scoop eggplant, tomatoes, and onions out of their skins before placing them in a soup pot. Squeeze garlic out of cloves before adding to pot. Add broth and thyme. Bring mixture to a boil and simmer 45 minutes.

Purée ingredients in a blender or food processor. At this point, soup can be refrigerated in a covered container until the next day.

When ready to serve, return soup to pot and heat gently to a simmer. Stir in half and half. Serve in wide rimmed bowls and garnish with crumbled feta cheese.

Serves 8 to 10

Spring Vegetable Soup

AS REFRESHING AS A WARM DAY IN SPRING, THIS WONDERFUL SOUP
IS JUST THE THING FOR ASPARAGUS SEASON.

1 bunch green onions, white part only

1 carrot

1 tablespoon butter

8 creamer white **or** red potatoes, quartered

1 can (14½ ounces) chicken broth **or** 1¾ cups homemade stock

½ cup frozen petite peas, thawed

1 cup asparagus tips, sliced

½ cup Pinot Grigio wine **or** water (optional)

Slice onions crosswise into ¼-inch pieces; peel and dice carrot. Heat butter over medium-low heat and add onions and carrots. Sauté until carrots are soft, about 5 minutes.

Add potatoes and stock. Bring to a boil and simmer until potatoes are soft, about 15 minutes.

Add peas, asparagus, and wine, water, or more stock, as desired. Heat to boiling and serve.

Makes 4 to 6 servings

Home gardeners can add to Spring Vegetable Soup tiny creamer potatoes (once called "new potatoes" because they could be pulled up at the same time as peas and carrots). These vegetables are also available year-round at farmers' markets, specialty stores, and even supermarkets. If unexpected company arrives, just add more stock to stretch the soup.

Peas lose their sugar to starch the minute they are picked. For freshest, sweetest flavors, use frozen peas. When you find fresh peas in the pod at farmers' markets, don't hesitate. Buy them and serve them raw as an appetizer or a healthy afternoon snack. Include a bowl for the empty pods.

Clam Chowder

FOR GREAT AMBIENCE, PREPARE VEGETABLES AHEAD OF TIME AND
PLAN TO PUT YOUR CHOWDER TOGETHER AND COOK IT OVER AN
OPEN FIRE AT A BEACH. WHILE YOU WATCH THE POT, IT'S FUN
TO SIP ON A GOOD PINOT GRIGIO.

4 strips bacon

2 medium potatoes

1 onion, chopped

2 stalks celery, sliced

1 large carrot, shredded **or** diced

1 bottle clam juice

2 cans chopped clams

1 cup half and half

¼ cup chopped parsley

Slice bacon crosswise into ½-inch strips. Peel potatoes and cut into ½-inch cubes.

In a heavy cast pot, fry bacon until crisp, removing any excess fat. Add onion and celery and sauté until onion is soft, about 5 minutes. Add carrot, clam juice, clams, and potatoes. Bring to a boil, cover, and simmer until potatoes are soft, about 10 to 15 minutes. Add half and half. Serve with a topping of chopped parsley.

Serves 4

Pacific Rim Chicken Broth

KEEPING YOUR OWN CHICKEN BROTH ON HAND NOT ONLY MAKES IT EASY
TO PLAN MEALS FEATURING SOUP, BUT IT'S ALSO A GOOD BASE FOR DISHES
WITH GINGER, CILANTRO, SOY, FISH SAUCE, SESAME OIL, OR HOT CHILES.
THIS BROTH IS LOW FAT AND CAN BE MADE WITHOUT SALT.

1 whole chicken

1 2-inch piece fresh ginger root

2 cloves garlic

1 stalk celery

3 pieces star anise (optional)

1 green onion

3 quarts cold water

1 teaspoon salt, if desired

To make a low-fat broth, keep the temperature just below boiling. Boiling incorporates the fat into the liquid and the fat doesn't rise, so you can't remove it.

Freeze some chicken broth in ice cube trays for occasions when a small amount of broth is needed.

Letting chicken cool in the broth adds juice and flavors to the chicken meat, making the chicken tender and tasty.

Wash chicken and trim fat. Place in a large stock pot. Peel ginger root, crush, and add to pot. Lightly crush garlic, trim ends, and peel before adding to the pot.

Add celery, star anise, onion, water, and salt to the pot. Turn heat up to high and cook until bubbles rise, about 10 minutes. Then turn heat down to lowest setting and simmer, not boil, for 1 hour or until meat is tender before turning off heat.

Let chicken cool in broth about 1 hour. Broth temperature should be above 150°. Remove chicken from broth and refrigerate chicken for later use.

Pour broth through a colander to remove seasonings. Refrigerate broth overnight. Next day, skim off fat. Place broth in freezer containers and freeze for up to 3 months.

Makes 3 quarts

Napa Cabbage Salad

A SHARP KNIFE OR A FOOD PROCESSOR WILL MAKE QUICK WORK

OF SLICING ALL VEGETABLES. PALE GREEN NAPA CABBAGE

TASTES LIKE A CROSS BETWEEN CELERY AND CABBAGE.

1 medium head napa cabbage

1 bunch **each** cilantro and radishes

4 green onions

½ green pepper (optional)

¼ cup toasted slivered almonds

Asian Low-fat Dressing:

2 tablespoons rice vinegar

1½ teaspoons sugar

¼ teaspoon powdered ginger

1 teaspoon sesame oil

1 teaspoon soy sauce

Mix ingredients together in a small bowl or jar. Makes enough dressing for a single recipe of Napa Cabbage Salad.

Mayonnaise-based Dressing:

½ cup mayonnaise

1 teaspoon **each** powdered ginger and sugar

1 tablespoon **each** soy sauce and rice vinegar

1 teaspoon sesame oil

Mix ingredients together in a small bowl or jar. Makes enough dressing for Napa Cabbage Salad.

Shred cabbage. Separate large stems from cilantro and discard; coarsely chop leaves. Thinly slice radishes and onions. Slice pepper into thin strips. Mix vegetables together in a serving bowl and add one of the Asian Dressings (see left). Just before serving, toss slivered almonds into the salad.

Serves 4 to 6

These dressings are wonderful for napa cabbage, bean sprouts, and rice salads. The low- acid content of rice wine vinegar and the balance of sugar complements Italian varietal white wines. Make dressings fresh each time and dress your salad lightly.

Roast Chicken Salad

THIS ATTRACTIVE COLD SALAD IS A WONDERFUL CHOICE
FOR A COMPANY LUNCHEON. IT CAN BE ARRANGED ON A SERVING PLATTER
OR ON INDIVIDUAL PLATES. ENJOY IT WITH A BOTTLE OF TOCAI FRIULANO
OR PINOT GRIGIO.

1 whole roast chicken, home-roasted **or** purchased

1 cup red cabbage, shredded

1 cup white cabbage, shredded

2 scallions (green onions), thinly sliced

¾ cup Sherry-Walnut Dressing (see recipe in box at right)

2 heads Belgian endive

16 slices fresh honeydew melon, peeled

1 head red leaf **or** butter lettuce, cleaned and leaves separated

2 oranges, peeled and cut into skinless segments

1 cup red grapes (optional)

Remove chicken from skin and bone; shred into pieces. Toss with shredded red and white cabbage, scallions, and ½-cup Sherry-Walnut Dressing. At this point, salad may be refrigerated until ready to be assembled.

Cut root end from endive and separate leaves. Arrange endive leaves and melon slices in a concentric circle on a platter or on individual plates. Place lettuce leaves in center of plate. Mound chicken salad in center of plate on lettuce leaves. Garnish with orange segments and grapes and drizzle with remaining ¼-cup dressing.

Serves 4

> ### Sherry-Walnut Dressing
>
> 1 teaspoon minced shallots
>
> 2 tablespoons sherry wine vinegar
>
> 2 tablespoons orange juice
>
> 1 teaspoon Dijon mustard
>
> 1 tablespoon honey
>
> 1 cup olive oil
>
> ½ cup walnut oil
>
> ¼ teaspoon *each* salt and white pepper
>
> *Mix ingredients thoroughly.*
>
> *Makes 1¾ cups dressing*

Smoked Chicken & Bosc Pear Salad

THE FLAVOR AND CRUNCHY TEXTURE OF BOSC PEARS MAKE A
WONDERFUL FOIL FOR THE SMOKED CHICKEN AND BLOOD ORANGE DRESSING.
IF YOU HAVE A HOME SMOKER, USE FRUIT WOOD FOR
SMOKING YOUR CHICKEN. THIS DISH IS DELIGHTFUL WHEN PAIRED
WITH PINOT GRIGIO.

1 head Romaine lettuce

1 head green leaf lettuce

2 Bosc pears

4 smoked chicken breasts **or** ¾ pound
deli-smoked chicken

Dressing:

4 tablespoons blood orange juice **or**
fresh orange juice

1 tablespoon Dijon mustard

2 tablespoons olive oil **or** salad oil

Salt and pepper to taste

Make dressing by whisking orange
juice, mustard, olive oil, salt, and
pepper together.

Wash and crisp lettuce. Wash and core pears and cut them into slices about ¼-inch-thick. Cut smoked chicken lengthwise into thinly sliced pieces.

Combine lettuce, place on plate, and arrange smoked chicken and Bosc pear slices on top. Drizzle dressing over all.

Serves 6

Crisp lettuce by immersing leaves in a deep bowl or large pan of cold water. Plunge leaves under water for a few minutes, then lift leaves from water, tear into pieces, and dry in a salad spinner.

Place a dry paper towel in plastic bag. Fill bag loosely with lettuce, top with another paper towel, and close bag tightly. Refrigerate a minimum of 4 hours. Lettuce is ready to use in salads.

Use this same method for cleaning the sand from spinach or parsley. Sometimes it may take two rinses to do the job.

Sweet Beet Salad

THIS COLORFUL DO-AHEAD RECIPE

IS A SURE WINNER FOR SALAD-ON-DEMAND.

1 bunch large beets

2 tablespoons raspberry vinegar

½ pound mixed salad greens

Vinaigrette dressing

4 ounces feta cheese, crumbled

Wash sand from beets. Cut top and root off. Place whole beets on foil-lined cookie sheet. Bake in a preheated oven at 450° for 1 hour. Cool and peel.

Julienne beets into ¼-inch strips. Toss beets with the raspberry vinegar and refrigerate up to 5 days.

To make the beet salad, lightly dress mixed greens with your favorite vinaigrette dressing; toss to mix. Place greens on salad plate, add beets, and garnish with feta cheese.

Serves 6

Roasting beets brings out their sweet flavor. When you roast beets for a warm side dish, put in more than you need. Then use the rest in this salad. The proportions can easily be multiplied to serve more people.

Save beet tops for cooked greens. Wash and cut crosswise into 2-inch pieces. Place stems in the bottom of a saucepan and leafy greens above. Add ¼-cup water, bring to a boil, and simmer until just tender, about 5 minutes.

To serve hot, simply sprinkle with your favorite vinegar. Or you can serve greens chilled and topped with yoghurt.

Canelli Bean Salad

ATTRACTIVE TO THE EYE, THIS BEAN SALAD IS SIMPLY GREAT TO TAKE
ON A PICNIC OR SERVE ON AN APPETIZER SMALL PLATE (PAGE 28).

1 cup dried Canelli **or** white beans, soaked, **or** 2 (15 ounce) cans, drained

⅓ cup extra virgin olive oil

¼ cup rice wine vinegar **or** white balsamic vinegar

1 tablespoon Dijon mustard

2 teaspoons **each** dry oregano leaves and fennel seeds

1 cup diced red bell pepper **or** mixed red and yellow pepper

¼ cup slivered fresh basil

¼ cup sliced green onion

¼ teaspoon **each** salt and pepper

¼ cup finely chopped parsley

1 head lettuce, red **or** green leaf, washed and crisped

In a pot, cover dried beans in water and cook until tender but not mushy, about 40 minutes. Drain and set aside.

In a large bowl, combine olive oil, vinegar, mustard, oregano, and fennel. Add red pepper, basil, onion, beans, salt, and pepper. Mix together and refrigerate at least 4 hours and up to 2 days to let flavors blend.

Just before serving, stir in chopped parsley. Line a salad bowl with lettuce and pile beans on top.

Serves 6

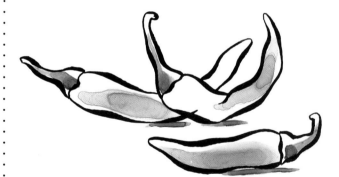

Cranberry Vinaigrette Salad

A TANGY DRESSING FOR A SALAD OF MIXED GREENS.

PINOT GRIGIO, ARNEIS, OR TOCAI FRIULANO

BLENDS BEAUTIFULLY WITH THIS TASTY FIRST-COURSE.

2 tablespoons extra virgin olive oil

4 tablespoons cranberry juice concentrate

2 tablespoons rice wine vinegar

1 teaspoon Dijon mustard

Salt and pepper

6 cups salad greens

Dried cranberries, toasted pecan halves, and slivered Asiago cheese for garnish

Put olive oil, cranberry juice, vinegar, mustard, salt, and pepper in a jar and shake well. Refrigerate up to 3 days.

Lightly dress salad greens. Garnish with cranberries, pecans, and cheese.

Serves 4 to 6

Use the highest quality hazelnut oil for Lemon Hazelnut Dressing. The subtle nut flavor and lemon juice enliven the salad and the pine nuts add a flavorful crunch. Dress salad lightly.

Canned chipolte peppers can be found in specialty markets or Mexican food stores. To add more heat to the dressing, add sauce from can to taste.

Lemon Hazelnut Dressing

THIS NUTTY-FLAVORED DRESSING IS WONDERFUL

FOR SPINACH AND DELICATE SALAD GREENS.

1 pound baby spinach, spinach, **or** spring mix

4 tablespoons hazelnut oil (see box on page 40) **or** pecan oil

2 tablespoons fresh lemon juice

⅛ teaspoon fresh ground nutmeg (optional)

¼ cup toasted pine nuts (optional)

Wash spinach and crisp.

Whisk hazelnut oil and lemon juice together and pour over greens. Toss lightly to mix.

Serves 4

Chipolte Dressing

THIS IS JUST THE RIGHT TOUCH TO DRESS FISH OR CHICKEN SALADS.

2 tomatoes

1 chipolte pepper, canned (see box on page 40)

¾ cup rice vinegar

1½ cups salad oil

Salt and pepper to taste

Core and cut tomatoes in half and place, cut side up, in a 450° oven. Roast 30 to 40 minutes. Cool before peeling.

In a food processor or blender, purée tomatoes, pepper, and vinegar together. Slowly add oil to combine ingredients.

Makes 1 quart dressing

Summer Eggplant Sandwich

NO NEED TO WORRY ABOUT BREAD WHEN YOU HAVE EGGPLANT
FOR YOUR SANDWICH. EASY TO ASSEMBLE AND DELICIOUS TO TASTE,
THIS RECIPE MAY BECOME YOUR SUMMER FAVORITE.

1 large eggplant

Salt

2 ripe medium tomatoes

5-6 slices fresh **or** block Mozzarella
  cheese

10-12 leaves of fresh basil

2 eggs

Flour, seasoned flour **or** breadcrumbs

Salad **or** olive oil

Freshly ground black pepper

Peel eggplant and cut into ¼-inch slices. Sprinkle well with salt and allow to stand for 30 minutes in a strainer with a bowl underneath. The salt draws out liquid. While the eggplant is sitting, cut thin slices of tomato and cheese; pick basil leaves.

Crack eggs into a bowl and beat gently. Place flour in a separate bowl. Rinse eggplant in cold water and pat dry.

Preheat oven or toaster oven to 350°.

Place one eggplant slice into beaten egg, then roll in flour to coat. Shake off excess. Repeat with remaining slices, placing them on sheet pan lined with wax paper. Pour a small amount of oil into a large sauté pan and heat over medium flame. Add a few eggplant slices at a time to the pan without crowding; brown 1 to 2 minutes on each side. Remove to another sheet pan. Add more oil, if necessary, for remaining eggplant.

Assemble sandwiches by topping an eggplant slice with one slice of tomato, a sprinkle of salt and black pepper, one or two basil leaves, and one slice of cheese. Cover with another eggplant slice.

When all the sandwiches are made, pop them into oven for 5 to 7 minutes to cook eggplant and melt cheese.

Serve hot or cold.

Makes 8 to 10 sandwiches

Spaghetti Squash

A DELIGHTFUL VEGETABLE DISH TO ACCOMPANY EITHER GRILLED OR ROASTED MEATS. HAZELNUT OIL AND ROASTED NUTS ADD TASTE APPEAL.

1 medium spaghetti squash

3 tablespoons high quality hazelnut oil

¼ cup chopped roasted filberts (optional)

Wash squash well. With a fork, poke many holes through shell into the interior.

Place squash in a microwave oven and cook on high for 4 minutes. Carefully turn squash and cook another 4 minutes, or until squash is soft all the way around. Remove from oven and let cool for 10 minutes.

Slice squash in half and remove seeds. Fluff strands of squash meat and place on serving plates or in a bowl. Drizzle with hazelnut oil and sprinkle with roasted filberts. Serve hot.

Serves 6

Avocado & Hazelnut Oil

For an easy starter course, slice an avocado in half. Remove seed and cut a flat spot on the bottom of each half so they will sit straight on plates. Fill cavities with hazelnut oil; garnish with wedges of lime.

Grandma's Green Beans

GREEN BEANS TAKE ON A WONDERFUL FLAVOR WHEN SLOW COOKED
ON THE BACK OF THE STOVE. THEY ALSO REHEAT WELL.
SERVE WITH ROASTED MEATS AND SANGIOVESE.

1 pound green beans, Kentucky
Wonder **or** Blue Lake

2 slices bacon

½ small yellow **or** red onion, diced

¼ cup catsup **or** chili sauce

½ cup water

Wash and trim both ends off beans. Cut into 2-inch lengths.

Cut bacon slices ½-inch crosswise. Brown bacon over medium heat in a saucepan. Discard fat.

Add onion to bacon; sauté until lightly brown. Add catsup, then beans, and stir to coat. Add water and simmer until beans are very tender, about 1 hour. Add more water if beans become dry.

Serves 4 to 6

Garlic Mashed Potatoes

ROASTED GARLIC ADDS A NUTTY FLAVOR AND AN EXCELLENT TEXTURE
TO MASHED POTATOES. THIS SIDE DISH CAN BE PREPARED IN
ADVANCE AND KEPT WARM, OR REFRIGERATED AND REHEATED.

4 medium baking potatoes, peeled and cut into ¾-inch chunks

1 teaspoon butter **or** margarine

1 head roasted garlic (see box below)

3 tablespoons sour cream, regular **or** fat free

1 teaspoon dried mustard

¾ teaspoon salt

¼ teaspoon white pepper

Boil potatoes over medium heat until fork-tender, about 20 minutes. Drain water from potatoes after cooking. Add butter to potatoes; mash potatoes with an electric mixer until there are no lumps.

Starting at the bottom of the garlic head, squeeze individual cloves into a bowl. Mash garlic cloves with the back of a fork until texture is consistent. Add sour cream, mustard, salt, and pepper to garlic. Stir to combine.

Add garlic mixture to potatoes; whip with an electric mixer until the texture is smooth. If you prefer a creamier texture, add additional sour cream.

Serves 4 to 6

To roast garlic, peel excess papery skin and roots from the head. With a sharp knife, cut 1/4- inch off the top of the garlic. Place garlic on a foil-lined baking sheet.

Preheat oven to 350°. Roast garlic for 45 minutes, or until soft and lightly browned. If you roast a number of garlic heads at one time, you can keep them refrigerated for a week or freeze them for later use.

Layered Zucchini & Potatoes

THIS DISH CAN BE USED AS AN INTERMEDIATE COURSE OR SERVED WITH
A MEAT ENTRÉE. A FAVORITE WITH PEOPLE WHO PREFER TO COOK
IN ADVANCE, THIS EASY VEGETABLE COMBO CAN BE MADE AS MUCH AS
TWO DAYS AHEAD, REFRIGERATED, AND REHEATED.

3 medium-large potatoes, such as Yukon Gold

3 medium zucchini

1 cup Tomato Sauce (page 50) **or** commercial marinara sauce

1 cup freshly grated Parmesan cheese

1 tablespoon **each** minced parsley and garlic, mashed together

Slice potatoes about ¼-inch thick in a food processor or with a sharp knife. Rinse slices in a bowl of water until the water is clear. Drain.

Microwave potatoes 3 to 7 minutes on high (time varies, depending on the microwave) until soft but not crumbly.

Slice zucchini crosswise in a food processor or cut with a sharp knife about ¼-inch thick.

Spread ¼-cup tomato sauce in the bottom of a medium (6- x 9-inch) rectangular casserole. Layer half of the potatoes on top of sauce; add a layer of zucchini on top of potatoes. Drizzle with ¼-cup tomato sauce, then sprinkle ½-cup Parmesan cheese over sauce. Repeat layers of potato, zucchini, and tomato sauce.

Scatter parsley-garlic mixture over top and add remaining Parmesan cheese. At this point, you can cover and refrigerate, up to 2 days, until ready to bake.

Bake the dish for 40 minutes at 375° or until the Parmesan cheese forms a slightly browned crust.

Serves 4 to 6

Baby Bok Choy

A QUICK COLD-WEATHER DISH, THIS SIMPLE TREATMENT OF BABY
BOK CHOY WOULD BE GOOD TO SERVE WITH ASIAN-FLAVORED
CHICKEN OR FISH. DON'T OVERCOOK THE BOK CHOY.

4 baby bok choy

2-inch piece fresh ginger root

4 cups water

½ teaspoon sesame oil

Toasted sesame seeds (optional)

Slice each bok choy in half lengthwise, keeping leaves attached to stems. Peel ginger and slice crosswise into 4 rounds.

In a wide saucepan, bring water to a boil, and add ginger and sesame oil. Place bok choy into boiling water, stem ends down, leaving tops above the water. Cook, covered, for 3 minutes. Drain, remove ginger, and place in serving bowl. Top with toasted sesame seeds, if desired.

Serves 4

Carrots, fresh asparagus, and sugar snap peas are also good candidates for the ginger-sesame cooking method described in the recipe. Carrots take a little longer than bok choy, but cook them until just tender. Both asparagus and whole sugar snap peas should be cooked until they turn bright green.

Baked Beans Plus

THAT ALL-AMERICAN FAVORITE, BAKED BEANS, TAKES ON A DIFFERENT
TEXTURE AND FLAVOR WHEN MADE WITH A DIFFERENT TYPE OF BEAN.
THIS DISH CAN BE USED AS AN APPETIZER SPREAD
OR AS A SIDE DISH FOR MEATS AND VEGETABLES. ALL YOU NEED
IS AN OVEN-PROOF POT WITH A LID.

½ pound dry Canelli beans

2 sprigs sage

2 tablespoons extra virgin olive oil

1 tablespoon minced garlic

¼ teaspoon salt

Sort beans for rocks. Cover with water and soak overnight or use the quick-cook method of bringing beans to a boil and simmering until just tender. Drain beans and rinse well.

In a ceramic or cast-iron, oven-proof pot, add cooked beans, sage, olive oil, garlic, and salt. Add water to cover beans. Stir to mix and cover. Place in a 200° oven and cook 6 to 8 hours, until beans are very soft and mushy.

Remove sage and serve beans warm, or refrigerate them up to 3 days. Reheat in microwave before serving.

Serves 6

For an easy appetizer, whip beans in a food processor, adding more extra virgin olive oil to taste. Serve at room temperature on crackers or toasted pita bread.

To toast pita bread, cut bread in half, then cut into 6 triangular pieces. Separate bread into single pieces and place on a cookie sheet. Bake in a 400° oven until crisp and brown, about 5 minutes.

Purely Potatoes

THIS SNACK IS A VEGETARIAN'S DELIGHT.

2 pounds unpeeled potatoes, russet, Yukon gold, white, or blue

Olive oil **or** vegetable spray

Wash potatoes and slice crosswise ½-inch-thick.

Spray a cookie sheet with olive oil or vegetable oil. Place a single layer of potato slices on the sheet. Bake 30 minutes in a preheated 450° oven, or until brown and puffy.

Serves 4

Herbed Potatoes

ADD HERBS TO POTATOES BEFORE COOKING TO SPICE UP THEIR FLAVOR.

2 pounds unpeeled potatoes

2 tablespoons olive oil

1 teaspoon herb mix

Wash potatoes and slice crosswise ½-inch-thick. Toss with olive oil and herb mix.

Spray a cookie sheet with olive oil or vegetable oil. Place potato slices on the sheet in a single layer. Bake for 30 minutes in a preheated 450° oven, or until brown and puffy.

Serves 4

Low in fat and simplicity itself to prepare, both of these potato recipes can be eaten right out of the oven, like french fries, with catsup, or as a snack to dip in yoghurt and chives. They are also delicious when diced and added to soups or stews.

Tomato Sauce for All Seasons

USE THIS FLAVORFUL TOMATO SAUCE WHENEVER A RECIPE CALLS FOR
CANNED SAUCE, AS A BASE FOR PASTA SAUCE, OR TO FLAVOR SOUPS OR
STEWS. MAKE IT WHEN FRESH, VINE-RIPENED TOMATOES ARE
PLENTIFUL AT FARMERS' MARKETS AND IN GROCERY STORES AND
FREEZE IN 1-CUP QUANTITIES IN ZIP-LOCK PLASTIC BAGS TO USE ALL YEAR.

8 pounds vine-ripened tomatoes

2 tablespoons olive oil

1 large yellow onion, chopped

1 bunch parsley, chopped

3 medium cloves garlic, minced

2 large **or** 4 small bay leaves

Salt and pepper

Remove skins, seeds, and cores from tomatoes and chop tomatoes coarsely.

In a large sauté pan or stockpot, heat olive oil; add chopped onions and cook until soft, about 5 minutes. Add tomatoes, parsley, garlic, and bay leaves to the pan.

Cook tomato mixture about 10 minutes on medium-high heat, stirring to heat mixture evenly, until tomatoes begin to release their liquid. Reduce heat to medium, cover pan loosely, and continue simmering for about 30 minutes, stirring occasionally to keep from sticking. Season to taste with the salt and pepper.

Let cool before removing bay leaves. Purée sauce in a food processor or pass through a food mill, using the smallest size sieve, before refrigerating or freezing.

Makes 5 cups

PASTAS & GRAINS

Pastas and grains are very popular with today's health-conscious and time-challenged society. Add a green salad, crusty bread, and wine—presto, the perfect meal! Or make a dish ahead and pop it in the freezer to use later. We found a Linguini Primavera to melt in your mouth and a Penne & Pine Nut Pasta guaranteed to win rave reviews, or try the traditional Sunday Lasagne. Somewhere in this chapter is a wine-friendly recipe that will become a family favorite.

Penne & Pine Nut Pasta

ITALIAN SAUSAGE FLAVORS THIS HEARTY QUICK-TO-FIX PASTA DISH.

YOU MIGHT HAVE THE INGREDIENTS ON YOUR PANTRY SHELVES.

THE KEY TO FLAVOR IS THE QUALITY OF THE SAUSAGE AND THE OLIVE OIL.

FOR RAVE REVIEWS, SERVE WITH A MIXED GREEN SALAD, A CRUSTY BREAD

AND YOUR FAVORITE SANGIOVESE.

1 pound mild **or** hot Italian sausage

1 red **or** yellow onion, chopped

3 cloves garlic, chopped

1 red bell pepper, optional

1 can (28 ounces) sliced Italian pear tomatoes, drained

1 teaspoon dried basil **or** Italian herb mix

½ cup Sangiovese **or** red wine

1 pound package penne pasta

1 tablespoon fruity extra virgin olive oil

¼ cup toasted pine nuts

¼ cup parsley, coarsely chopped

Slice sausage crosswise into ½-inch rounds. Heat a large sauté pan, add sausage, and cook until brown, about 5 minutes. Transfer sausage to a bowl and pour off fat.

Cut pepper into 1-inch pieces.

Using the same pan, sauté onion, garlic, and red pepper in remaining browned bits until onion is soft, about 5 minutes. Return sausage to pan. Add tomatoes, basil, and wine. Cover and simmer 5 minutes or until pasta is ready.

Cook pasta according to package directions. Drain, place in heated bowl, and toss with olive oil.

Add pine nuts and parsley to sausage mixture. Stir to heat through and serve over warm pasta.

Serves 4 to 6

Toasted Pine Nuts

Preheat oven to 400°. Spread nuts on an aluminum pie pan (if toasting only a small amount) or a cookie sheet (if toasting a lot). Toast nuts in oven 5 to 10 minutes, stirring occasionally, until golden brown. Remove from heat.

(Nuts can also be toasted on top of the stove in a frying pan over medium heat. Stir continually until brown, but not burned. Remove from heat.)

Buy pine nuts in bulk, toast them all at once, and place them in freezer until needed.

Fresh Tomato Pasta

MAKE THIS FLAVORFUL PASTA WHEN VINE-RIPENED TOMATOES
COME ON THE MARKET. THE QUALITY OF EACH INGREDIENT IS IMPORTANT.
THIS DISH GOES WELL WITH SANGIOVESE, BARBERA OR NEBBIOLO.

4 large vine-ripened tomatoes, any color

2 cloves garlic

2 tablespoons extra virgin olive oil

1 bunch fresh basil

1 package (16 ounces) pasta, such as fusilli **or** penne

½ cup Parmigiano-Reggiano cheese, freshly grated

Cut tomatoes crosswise, remove seeds and dice coarsely. Place tomatoes into a non-corrosive bowl. With a garlic press, squeeze garlic juice over tomatoes and add 1 tablespoon olive oil. Stir gently to mix and set aside.

Separate and discard stems from basil. Pile basil leaves in a stack, then roll them up. With a sharp knife, make thin slices across the roll to make basil slivers. Repeat as needed. Set slivers aside.

Cook pasta according to package directions, drain, and place in a bowl. Toss pasta gently with remaining 1 tablespoon olive oil, basil, and tomatoes. Top with cheese.

Serves 4 to 6

Nutty Sauced Pasta

TOASTED SEEDS AND NUTS GIVE PASTA AN UNEXPECTED EXOTIC FLAVOR.

SERVE AS A FIRST COURSE WITH A DRY MOSCATO OR TOCAI FRIULANO, OR

AS A MAIN DISH WITH CRANBERRY VINAIGRETTE SALAD (PAGE 40),

SOFT BISCUITS, AND SANGIOVESE.

½ cup **each** pumpkin seeds and whole
  almonds

⅓ cup pine nuts

1 clove garlic

¼ teaspoon salt

⅛ teaspoon white pepper

1 cup half and half

1 package (1 pound) fettuccine

Lime wedges

Spread pumpkin seeds, almonds, and pine nuts on a cookie sheet. Place in a 350° oven until lightly browned, about 8 to 10 minutes. Let cool.

In a food processor or blender, combine nuts, garlic, salt, and pepper. Whirl until the texture of peanut butter before adding half and half. If made ahead, cover and refrigerate overnight. Bring to room temperature before using.

Cook pasta according to directions. Drain and immediately toss pasta lightly in sauce to coat. Pass lime wedges at table.

Makes 4 to 8 servings

Linguini Primavera

COLORFUL RESTAURANT AU PARMESAN IS JUST STEPS AWAY FROM THE FAMED
CHATEAU FRONTENAC IN QUEBEC CITY. WHEN ASKED A FAVORITE
RECIPE TO GO WITH A ROBUST SANGIOVESE, CO-OWNER LUIGI LEONI GAVE US
HIS VERSION OF A FAVORITE ITALIAN DISH.

½ cup diced red onion

3 zucchini

¼ pound green beans

1 head broccoli

1 cup chicken broth, homemade **or** canned low-sodium

1 cup tomato sauce

2 tomatoes, peeled, seeded, and chopped

¼ cup chopped basil **or** 2 tablespoons dry

1 tablespoon mint leaves **or** 1 teaspoon dry

Salt and pepper to taste

1 16 ounce package linguini

Parmigiano-Reggiano **or** Parmesan cheese for topping

Cook onion in microwave for 1 minute. Trim ends of zucchini and cut into quarters lengthwise. Cut again crosswise into ½-inch triangles. Slice beans into ½-inch pieces. Pull broccoli apart into small buds. Cook zucchini, beans, and broccoli separately 2 minutes each in microwave, just until bright green.

In a large sauté pan, heat chicken broth and tomato sauce. Boil to reduce liquid by half, about 3 minutes.

Add vegetables, tomatoes, basil, and mint. Bring to a boil, stirring gently, until heated through and bubbly. Salt and pepper to taste. Turn off heat, cover, and serve with pasta as soon as it is cooked.

Cook pasta al dente, according to package directions. Drain, top with sauce and cheese.

Serves 4

Travel Tip

Nightly accordion music, waiters who burst into operatic arias or popular French tunes, and over 2,000 intricately shaped liqueur bottles decorating every nook and cranny—it's all part of the charm of Restaurant au Parmesan, 38 rue St. Louis, in Quebec City's upper Old Town. But it's the food that keeps customers returning to this eatery, recently named one of the world's 100 Best Italian Restaurants. We agree and so do the celebrities whose photos line the walls.

Sunday Lasagne

DON'T UNDERESTIMATE THE POWER OF GOOD LASAGNE!
BUT LIKE ANY SUNDAY OR HOLIDAY DINNER, THIS DISH TAKES A LITTLE
TIME TO FIX. YOU MIGHT WANT TO INVITE ONE OF YOUR CHILDREN
OR A FAMILY MEMBER TO HELP. START EARLY AND ENJOY YOUR TIME
TOGETHER IN THE KITCHEN. IT'S MORE THAN JUST FOOD; THIS SHARED
MEAL CAN BECOME A HIGHLY VALUED PART OF FAMILY LIFE,
LINKING TODAY'S COOKS WITH GENERATIONS PAST.

Meat Sauce:

1 tablespoon olive oil

4 cloves garlic, mashed

1 small onion, diced

6 ounces Italian sausage

6 ounces ground sirloin **or** turkey

1 tablespoon Italian herbs

1 can (28 ounces) Italian tomatoes, crushed

1 small zucchini, diced (optional)

1 cup Sangiovese **or** Barbera

Cheese Sauce:

1 container (15 ounces) ricotta cheese

8 ounces Mozzarella cheese, shredded

4 tablespoons grated Parmigiano-Reggiano **or** Parmesan cheese

¼ cup fresh Italian flat leaf parsley, chopped

1 egg

Preparing Meat Sauce:

Heat olive oil on medium-low heat and cook garlic until browned; remove garlic and discard. Add onion and cook until translucent, about 2 to 3 minutes. Add sausage and ground meat. Cook and chop with a wooden spoon until very fine and well cooked. Add herbs; stir for 1 minute. Add tomatoes, zucchini, and wine. Simmer until meat is tender and sauce is reduced, about 20 minutes.

Preparing Cheese Sauce:

Combine ricotta cheese and 1 cup of shredded Mozzarella cheese, Parmesan cheese, parsley, and egg. Blend with a spoon and place in refrigerator.

Homemade Pasta:

3½ cups semolina **or** bread flour

4 extra-large eggs, slightly beaten

1 tablespoon olive oil

Mixing the pasta:

Pour 3 cups flour into a bowl. Make a well in the middle of the flour large enough for all the eggs. Add olive oil. With your hands, slowly mix the flour into the eggs to create a batter. Don't worry if it looks like a hopelessly messy lump. Knead the dough on a floured breadboard or counter top for about 3 minutes. Its consistency should be elastic and a little sticky. If too dry, add water a few sprinkles at a time; if too sticky, add more flour.

Knead for 10 minutes or until the dough becomes satiny, smooth, and very elastic. Do not try to save time on this step; it is important! Wrap dough in plastic and set aside to rest.

Rolling the pasta:

Sprinkle counter top with flour. Shape ¼ of the dough into a ball and roll out with your largest rolling pin. Slowly stretch the dough into a sheet of even thickness, as thinly as possible, to fit your pan. If necessary, cut with a knife to fit. Roll each layer of pasta, one at a time, as you need them.

Assembly:

Rub a 9- x 13-inch glass or porcelain casserole pan with olive oil. Lay a sheet of pasta into your pan, followed by a thin layer of meat, and then cover with a layer of cheese. Ration your ingredients so that you can get three layers—ending with a layer of meat sauce. Top with the remaining shredded Mozzarella and bake at 350° or until hot, bubbling, and browned on top, about 45 minutes.

Serves 6 to 8

Mushroom Risotto

RISOTTO IS A GOOD MAKE-AHEAD MAIN COURSE OR SIDE DISH.
SIMPLY REHEAT IT IN A MICROWAVE OVEN, OR TIGHTLY COVER AND
PLACE IN A 350° CONVENTIONAL OVEN FOR 30 MINUTES.

2 cups sliced portobello **or** shiitake mushrooms

2 tablespoons butter

1 tablespoon olive oil

3 cloves garlic, minced

1 small onion, diced

2 cups Arborio **or** short-grain rice, uncooked

10-20 saffron strands, soaked in ½-cup warm water

1 cup Pinot Grigio **or** white wine

2 cups beef **or** vegetable broth

Sauté mushrooms in 1 tablespoon of butter until brown, about 5 minutes. Set aside.

In a saucepan over medium heat, heat remaining butter and olive oil. Add garlic and onion. After cooking the onions and garlic for about 2 minutes, add rice and stir to heat and coat with oil. Cook until onions are translucent, about 2 more minutes.

Add saffron water and wine to rice, stirring constantly. Heat beef broth to a near boil.

As the rice mixture begins to thicken, add beef broth, a little at a time. Continue to add broth, stirring constantly. The liquid should become almost creamy in appearance and texture while the rice still holds its shape. Continue to stir. After 15 minutes, taste the risotto to see if the rice is done. If you need more liquid, use water heated to almost boiling, or any heated stock.

Add mushrooms to risotto mixture and allow to heat.

Serves 6

Cool Rice

THIS REFRESHING VEGETABLE-PACKED RICE GOES WELL WITH
WHITE AND RED WINES FROM MUSCAT CANELLI TO BARBERA.
YOU CAN SERVE IT COLD OR AT ROOM TEMPERATURE.
IT'S ALSO A GOOD TAKE-ALONG DISH FOR PICNICS.

1⅔ cup water

¼ teaspoon salt

1 cup long-grain brown rice

1 medium cucumber

1 cup cooked corn kernels (cut from 2 ears of corn), white **or** yellow

1 large tomato, seeded and diced

½ cup minced parsley

1 teaspoon minced sage **or** ¼ teaspoon dry

2 green onions (including tops), thinly sliced

1 jar (4½ ounces) pitted Kalamata olives, chopped **or** 1 can sliced black olives, drained

2 tablespoons extra virgin olive oil

1 tablespoon balsamic vinegar

1 teaspoon Dijon mustard

¼ teaspoon salt

Olives, toasted almonds, tomato wedges, and parsley for garnish

In a medium saucepan, bring water and salt to a boil. Stir in rice, cover, and reduce heat to low. Simmer 40 minutes or until all liquid is absorbed. Remove from heat (do not stir) and let stand until cool.

Peel cucumber, cut in quarters lengthwise, and remove seeds; then cut crosswise into thin slices. In a bowl, combine cucumber, corn, tomato, parsley, sage, green onions, and ¾ of the olives, saving some for garnish.

Mix together olive oil, vinegar, mustard, and salt. Pour over vegetables. Fluff cooled rice with a fork, add to vegetables, and toss until evenly mixed. Cover and chill until serving time, up to 2 days. When ready to serve, garnish with olives, almonds, tomato wedges, and parsley.

Serves 6 to 8

If you have a rice cooker, cook rice according to cooker directions. After rice is cooked, follow recipe directions.

Frozen corn kernels may be substituted for fresh corn, if desired. You might enjoy also enjoy adding diced avocado to the vegetable mixture.

Baked Mushroom Polenta
with Asiago Cheese

THIS IS A GOOD MAKE-AHEAD MAIN DISH. YOU CAN PREPARE
THE POLENTA AND SAUCE ON ONE DAY, THEN ADD CHEESE
AND BAKE IT THE NEXT.

1 pound mushrooms, thickly sliced

4 cups chicken stock **and** 1½ cup water

1½ cups polenta **or** yellow cornmeal

⅓ cup grated Parmesan cheese

½ teaspoon salt

½ teaspoon white pepper

3 large shallots, finely chopped

2 large cloves garlic, minced

1 cup Pinot Grigio **or** white wine

1 can (28 ounces) crushed tomatoes

1 teaspoon minced fresh thyme **or** ½ teaspoon dry thyme

Pinch of sugar

2 medium roasted red **and** yellow bell peppers, peeled and cut in squares

2 tablespoons fresh Italian parsley, minced

8 ounces Asiago **or** Mozzarella cheese, shredded

Cook mushrooms over medium heat in a frying pan coated with vegetable spray or olive oil until browned, about 10 minutes. Set aside.

In a heavy saucepan, bring chicken stock and water to a boil. Whisk in cornmeal until smooth and cook until tender and pulling away from the sides of the pan, about 30 minutes. Stir in mushrooms, 2 tablespoons Parmesan cheese, salt, and pepper. Spread the polenta into a 9- x 13-inch baking dish. If you plan to cook the polenta later, let cool and refrigerate until ready to use.

In a saucepan, combine shallots, garlic, wine, tomatoes, thyme, and sugar. Bring to a boil and simmer, uncovered, until reduced by half, about 30 minutes. Add peppers and parsley. If you plan to use the sauce later, cool and refrigerate.

When ready to eat polenta, preheat oven to 375°. Pour sauce over polenta. Combine remaining Parmesan cheese with Asiago and sprinkle over sauce. Bake 30 minutes or until hot and cheeses are melted and browned. Cut into squares or triangles and serve.

Serves 8 to 10

Thin Crust Olive Pizza

THIS NICELY SEASONED VEGETABLE PIZZA IS GOOD AS A MAIN DISH OR
CAN BE CUT INTO SMALL PIECES FOR APPETIZERS. YOU MAY FIND ITALIAN
TOMATOES UNDER THE NAME OF ROMA TOMATOES. OPEN A REFOSCO OR
MOSCATO CANELLI AND ENJOY COMPLIMENTS FROM FRIENDS.

5 fresh Italian tomatoes

1 small red onion, thinly sliced

½ pound mushrooms, white, brown, **or** shiitake, sliced

1 Anaheim pepper **or** 1 small green bell pepper

1 package commercial refrigerated pizza crust

1 jar (4½ onces) pitted Kalamata olives **or** 1 can sliced olives

1 tablespoon fresh basil, slivered **or** 1 teaspoon dry

1 teaspoon dry leaf oregano

½ teaspoon fennel **or** anise seed

2½ cups shredded Asiago **or** Mozzarella cheese

¾ cup grated dry Monterey jack cheese **or** Parmesan cheese

Cut tomatoes in half crosswise, remove seeds, and slice thinly. Set aside.

Place onion, mushrooms, and pepper in a microwave dish. Precook for about 3 minutes on high. Let cool; drain any excess juices.

Prepare pizza crust according to package instructions. Remove from oven and place tomatoes evenly on top of crust. Layer with cooked vegetables, olives, and fresh basil. Sprinkle oregano, fennel, and Asiago cheese over crust, then top with grated Monterey jack.

Return to oven and bake until cheese melts and top is brown, about 10 minutes.

Serves 4

The Franciscan missionaries, who were responsible for planting the first grape vines in California 200 years ago, also planted olive trees, which gave rise to a new industry.

The last decade has seen a renaissance in olive oil production. Today many boutique producers draw glistening gold and cool green oils from prized Manzanillo, Sevillano, Mission, and Picholine olives, which are grown throughout the state.

Couscous with Peppers, Onions & Herbs

A COLORFUL ADDITION TO GRILLED MEAT, THIS DISH CAN
ALSO STAND ON ITS OWN AS AN ENTRÉE. DRINK THE WINE
YOU COOK WITH, SUCH AS PINOT GRIGIO OR TOCAI FRIULANO.

½ yellow onion, finely diced

½ red bell pepper, finely diced

½ yellow bell pepper, finely diced

3 tablespoons garlic-flavored olive oil
(see box below)

1 cup water

1 cup vegetable broth, chicken stock,
or white wine

½ teaspoon salt

2 cups couscous **or** 1 package
(11 ounces)

2 tablespoons mixed, chopped, fresh
herbs, such as basil, thyme, and
parsley

Dice onion and peppers. Heat 1 tablespoon olive oil in a sauté pan. Cook vegetables until soft and lightly browned, about 4 minutes. Set aside.

Combine water, stock, remaining 2 tablespoons oil, and salt in a saucepan with a tightly fitting lid. Bring to a boil, stir in couscous, cover, and remove from heat. Let couscous sit for 5 minutes. Remove lid and transfer couscous to a larger bowl.

Using a fork, separate and fluff couscous grains. Stir in pepper-onion mixture and add herbs, adjusting seasoning, if needed. Couscous can be served warm or at room temperature.

Makes 6 cups

Garlic Olive Oil

1 head garlic
2 cups olive oil

Roughly chop garlic, skins and all. Put garlic into a saucepan and add olive oil. Bring oil to a simmer and cook on medium heat until garlic turns golden brown, 10 to 15 minutes. Cool before straining oil into a clean container. Using a funnel, transfer oil into a container from which it can be easily poured. Refrigerate.

For extra olive flavor, substitute 1 cup extra virgin oil for olive oil.

Oil can be used both for cooking and flavoring.

Lentil & Bulgur Wheat Pilaf

TRY TO FIND FRENCH GREEN LENTILS FOR THIS DISH IN SPECIALTY GROCERY
STORES OR ORDER THEM BY MAIL (SEE RESOURCE GUIDE, PAGE 110).
SERVE PILAF AS A SIDE DISH TO GRILLED MEATS,
AND POUR A GLASS OF SANGIOVESE OR BARBERA.

½ cup French green **or** regular lentils

2 cups water

2 tablespoons olive oil

1 medium onion, finely chopped

1 red **or** yellow bell pepper, diced

2 cloves garlic, chopped

½ teaspoon **each** ground allspice and cumin

1 cup bulgur wheat

1 teaspoon grated lemon peel

1½ cups chicken **or** vegetable broth

1 tablespoon lemon juice

¼ cup chopped mint **or** parsley

In a small pan, combine lentils and water. Bring to a boil, reduce heat, cover, and simmer until tender, about 15 minutes. Drain; set aside.

In a large sauté pan, heat olive oil. Add onion, bell pepper, and garlic. Sauté over medium heat until onion is soft and lightly brown, about 7 minutes. Add allspice, cumin, and bulgur. Cook, stirring to coat bulgur with onion and spices, for 1 minute more.

In a small pan, add lemon peel to broth and bring to a boil. Add broth to the bulgur mixture, stirring to mix. Cover sauté pan tightly and cook over low heat until broth is absorbed and bulgur is tender, about 5 minutes.

Stir in lentils, lemon juice, and mint; cook until mixture is heated through. Serve warm or at room temperature.

Serves 6

Moist Cornbread

USE FRESHLY GROUND WHOLE CORNMEAL FOR THIS MOIST SIDE BREAD.

IF YOU CAN'T FIND WHOLE CORNMEAL, CHECK OUR RESOURCE GUIDE,

PAGE 110. SERVE THIS BREAD WITH PASTA, SOUPS, BEANS,

OR SPICY MEATS.

2 cups cornmeal

1 teaspoon soda

¼ teaspoon salt (optional)

2 eggs

2 cups buttermilk **or** plain yoghurt

½ cup chopped red pepper (optional)

½ cup pine nuts (optional)

Preheat oven to 400°. Spray a 9-inch round cake pan with nonstick spray.

Mix cornmeal, salt, and soda. In a bowl, slightly beat eggs before adding buttermilk, cornmeal, and red pepper, if desired. Pour corn batter into pan. Sprinkle pine nuts on top and press lightly into batter. Bake 25 minutes or until cornbread is brown on top. Let bread sit for 5 minutes before cutting into pie-shaped wedges.

Makes 6 pieces

POULTRY & SEAFOOD

Sautéed, simmered, baked, or grilled—poultry lends itself to many cooking techniques. For more variety, we added exotic marinades, seasonings, and spicy fruit flavors. We encourage you to try poultry sausage with several easy-to-prepare recipes. Seafood lovers will find exciting new ways to serve Sautéed Prawns, Grilled Trout, Fish in Ginger-Wine Sauce, and several salmon dishes. Best of all, we include suggestions for exactly the right wine to accompany almost every entrée.

Parsley-Garlic Chicken

EASY TO MAKE AND QUICK TO PREPARE,

THIS ENTRÉE WORKS WELL WITH STEAMED VEGETABLES

AND PINOT GRIGIO OR TOCAI FRIULANO WINE.

4 medium boneless, skinless chicken breasts

1 tablespoon **each** butter and olive oil

2 tablespoons Parsley-Garlic Season ing (see box below)

½ cup Pinot Grigio **or** other white wine

Salt and pepper to taste

Parsley-Garlic Seasoning

2 tablespoons flat-leaf Italian parsley leaves, minced

2 medium cloves garlic, minced

To make small amounts of fresh seasoning, mince parsley and garlic with a sharp knife until they are reduced to a pulp.

For larger quantities, use a food processor to mince equal parts of garlic and parsley. Mix with a small amount of olive oil and refrigerate in a sealed container up to a week.

Trim excess fat from chicken breasts and pat them dry.

Using medium-high heat, melt butter and olive oil in a sauté pan. Brown chicken breasts for 1 to 2 minutes per side, then remove chicken from pan. The chicken will not be fully cooked.

Reduce the heat to medium and add Parsley-Garlic Seasoning and butter. Stir in any drippings from the chicken and wine to pick up all browned bits.

Add chicken breasts. Continue cooking chicken in sauce until all pink is gone from the center of the thickest chicken breast. Test by making a cut on the underside of the chicken or use a probe thermometer to test to 150°. Season to taste with salt and pepper.

Slice each chicken breast into three pieces, lengthwise. Distribute the sauce over the chicken. Serve on a platter family-style.

Serves 4

Apple Ginger Chicken

THE WONDERFUL SPICY FRUIT FLAVORS OF THIS MAIN DISH
PERFECTLY COMPLEMENT SANGIOVESE WINE. YOU MIGHT
WANT TO SPOON SAUCE OVER ORZO PASTA.

12 large chicken thighs, skin removed

½ teaspoon **each** salt, pepper, and
   paprika, mixed together

2 tablespoons olive oil

1 medium apple, such as Granny
   Smith, peeled, cored, and diced

1 teaspoon curry powder

½ teaspoon ground cinnamon

1 teaspoon **each** fresh thyme and
   minced ginger **or** ¼ teaspoon **each**
   dry thyme and ground ginger

¼ cup Major Grey's chutney, chopped

1 can (11 ounces) mandarin oranges

4 tablespoons chopped fresh mint

Sprinkle chicken with salt, pepper, and paprika. Heat olive oil in a large sauté or frying pan and brown chicken. Remove pieces when browned and place in a 9- x13-inch baking dish.

Reduce heat and add apple, curry powder, cinnamon, thyme, ginger, and chutney to sauté pan. Drain liquid from oranges into pan, reserving fruit. Cook mixture about 1 minute, stirring to pick up browned chicken bits.

Pour apple mixture over chicken and bake, uncovered, in a 350° oven for 45 minutes or until chicken is fork tender. Top with reserved oranges and 2 tablespoons mint. Bake 5 minutes longer. Remove from oven. Sprinkle remaining mint over chicken before serving.

Serves 6

Chicken & Dumplings

YELLOW, WHITE, OR RED POTATOES WORK WELL IN THIS ONE-DISH DINNER.

ADD A TOSSED GREEN SALAD AND OPEN A BOTTLE OF

SANGIOVESE OR BARBERA.

Chicken:

3 pounds boneless, skinless chicken thighs

1 tablespoon olive oil

2 tablespoons Hungarian sweet paprika

1¼ pounds red potatoes, unpeeled and cut into ½-inch dice

2 carrots, peeled and cut into ½-inch dice

1 medium onion, chopped

5-7 cloves garlic, slivered

1 red bell pepper, cut into ¼-inch dice

½ teaspoon salt

Pepper

Dumplings:

1½ cups pancake **or** biscuit mix

½ cup yellow cornmeal

⅔ cup milk

In a 5-quart Dutch oven, sauté chicken in oil until about half-cooked, 5-10 minutes. Sprinkle with paprika. Add potatoes, carrots, onion, garlic, and bell pepper. Barely cover with water. Cover pot, bring to a boil, and simmer 10 minutes. Season with salt and pepper to taste.

Combine pancake mix, cornmeal, and milk in a bowl. Stir lightly until dough forms a soft dumpling.

Using a large spoon, drop dumplings into simmering broth. Cook 10 minutes with cover off. Replace cover and simmer another 10 minutes. Serve at once.

Serves 6

If your family or company is late, place the covered Dutch oven in a 200° oven until ready to serve. Dumplings and stew will hold for 45 minutes. (This is also the technique you would use for "holding" other dishes.)

Marinated Grilled Chicken

MARINATING THE CHICKEN OVERNIGHT ADDS AN ASIAN FLAVOR
AND ALSO KEEPS THE CHICKEN FROM DRYING OUT WHILE BEING GRILLED.
THIS IS AN EASY RECIPE TO DOUBLE OR TRIPLE FOR LARGE GROUPS.

⅓ cup soy sauce

1 cup water

1 teaspoon sesame oil **or** 1 tablespoon crushed toasted sesame seed

2 cloves garlic, minced

¼ cup ginger, minced

2 green onions, thinly sliced

1 frying chicken, cut into pieces **or** 3
pounds chicken pieces

Combine soy sauce, water, sesame oil, garlic, ginger, and green onions. Place chicken pieces in a heavy-duty, zip-lock plastic bag or in a non-corrosive container. Pour marinade over chicken to cover and refrigerate overnight. Occasionally turn chicken pieces to thoroughly cover with marinade.

Prepare outdoor grill for indirect heat cooking. Cook chicken until meat near bone is no longer pink when slashed, about 40 to 60 minutes.

Serves 4

Poultry Sausage & Saucy Spinach

MANY SPECIALTY MEAT MARKETS MAKE THEIR OWN LOW-FAT, FRESH

SAUSAGE LINKS FROM A VARIETY OF POULTRY, SUCH AS CHICKEN, TURKEY,

AND DUCK. SOME ARE MILDLY SEASONED; OTHERS ARE QUITE HOT.

FOR MAXIMUM ENJOYMENT,

POUR A HEARTY BARBERA WITH THIS MEAL.

6 large fresh chicken **or** turkey
sausages

Spinach:

1 tablespoon **each** olive oil and butter

1 onion, sliced lengthwise into ¼-inch
pieces

1 clove garlic, chopped

1 tablespoon slivered fresh basil **or** 1
teaspoon dry basil

1 tomato, peeled, seeded, and
chopped

¼ cup Barbera **or** red wine

¼ teaspoon salt

¼ teaspoon **each** ground nutmeg and
white pepper

2 bunches spinach, washed and stems
removed

Lemon wedges, for garnish

Place sausages in a frying pan or sauté pan. Add ½-inch cold water to the pan and bring to a boil. Lower heat, and poach sausages for 3 minutes on each side. Drain water, and brown sausages in pan or on a grill.

In a large sauté pan, heat olive oil and butter. Add onion and garlic and cook until onion is soft and beginning to brown, about 5 minutes. Add basil and stir to mix. Add tomato, wine, salt, nutmeg, and pepper. Simmer until mixture is thick, stirring occasionally, about 3 minutes. Add spinach and continue cooking until spinach is wilted and thoroughly mixed with sauce.

To serve, place spinach on 6 pre-warmed plates. Top with a sausage and garnish with a lemon wedge.

Serves 6

Barbera Stew

THIS EASY-TO-PREPARE DISH COMBINES FRESH SAUSAGE
FROM YOUR MEAT MARKET WITH A NICELY SEASONED SAUCE.
SIMPLY SERVE WITH BOW TIE PASTA, A GREEN SALAD, AND A GLASS
OF BARBERA OR NEBBIOLO WINE.

2 pounds Italian hot **or** mildly seasoned fresh chicken **or** turkey sausage

4 red **or** yellow sweet peppers

4 large onions

1 can (15 ounces) tomato sauce

2 tablespoons leaf oregano

½ teaspoon anise **or** fennel seed

2 cups Barbera **or** other red wine

Cut sausages crosswise into 1-inch pieces. Remove seeds from peppers and cut into ½-inch pieces. Slice onions in half lengthwise; then cut crosswise into ¼-inch slices.

In a 6- to 8-quart pot, combine sausage, peppers, onion, tomato sauce, oregano, anise seed, and wine. Cover pot; bring to a boil, reduce heat, and simmer for 2 to 3 hours.

Serves 6

Travel Tip

San Luis Obispo has always been one of the central coast's most interesting towns. Its unusual landmarks include campy Madonna Inn, one of Frank Lloyd Wright's houses, an Andrew Carnegie library (now a museum), a Franciscan mission, a Chinese store that dates back to the 1800s, and Bubble Gum Alley, which locals have festooned with collections of Bazooka, Dentyne, Wrigley, and much more.

The town also has one of the state's best Farmers' Markets. Every Thursday night, from 6:30 to 9 p.m. during the growing season, downtown Higuera Street between Nipomo and Osos streets hosts a lively outdoor market. If you'd rather watch than buy, choose a seat in one of several cozy coffee houses nearby.

Sautéed Prawns

UNEXPECTED COMPANY COMING FOR DINNER?
SERVE THIS SPEEDY ENTRÉE WITH QUICK-COOKING EGG NOODLES AND FRESH
STEAMED VEGETABLES. SURPRISINGLY, RED WINE, SUCH AS SANGIOVESE, GOES
WELL WITH SHRIMP. TRADITIONALISTS FIND PINOT GRIGIO PLEASING.

1 pound (about 36 to a pound) large prawns, shelled and deveined

2 teaspoons cornstarch

½ teaspoon sesame oil

¼ teaspoon salt

⅛ teaspoon white pepper

Sauce:

½ cup wine

2 tablespoons catsup

1 tablespoon Worcestershire sauce

1 teaspoon dry mustard **or** Dijon mustard

1 teaspoon cornstarch

2 tablespoons olive **or** vegetable oil

3 cloves garlic, minced

1 tablespoon minced ginger

4 green onions with tops, thinly sliced

In a medium bowl, toss shrimp with cornstarch, sesame oil, salt, and pepper. Let stand 15 minutes.

Combine ingredients for sauce in a small bowl.

Heat olive oil in a sauté or frying pan over medium-high heat until hot. Add garlic and ginger; stir-fry for 10 seconds. Add shrimp and stir-fry until pink, 2 to 3 minutes. Add green onions and stir once.

Stir sauce before adding to pan. Cook, stirring, until sauce bubbles and thickens. Remove from heat and cover until ready to serve.

Serves 4

Apple Wood Grilled Trout

SMOKE AND TROUT FLAVORS GO TOGETHER, REMINDING ONE THAT FISHING FOR A STREAMSIDE MEAL WAS EASY NOT SO LONG AGO. NOW LOOK FOR FRESH TROUT IN YOUR FISH MARKET AND USE AN OUTDOOR GRILL OR SMOKER FOR THIS RECIPE.

4 trout fillets

Salt and pepper

1 bunch fresh thyme **or** ½ teaspoon dried

1 lemon

1 cup apple wood chips **or** other fruit wood chips, for grilling

Watercress and lemon wedges, for garnish

With a paper towel, remove moisture from trout fillets. Lay fillets, skin side down, on aluminum foil. Trim foil around trout, leaving foil about ½-inch larger than trout. Season trout with salt and pepper.

Strip leaves from thyme stems before distributing leaves evenly over fillets and pressing them into place. Squeeze lemon juice over fillets.

Heat grill with a medium fire. Cook trout, on foil, 8 to 10 minutes. The amount of smoke will determine the color. To serve, lift trout from skin and aluminum foil and place on a plate garnished with lemon wedges and watercress sprigs.

Serves 4

To get maximum smoke on a charcoal grill, place ½-cup chips directly on coals just before you place the trout on the grill. Close dampers almost all the way. Replenish as necessary. For a gas grill, put wood chips into an empty tuna can and place on the rocks.

Serena's Savory Salmon

WHETHER YOU CATCH IT YOURSELF OR BUY IT FROM YOUR FAVORITE
FISH MARKET, THIS MASKED SALMON TASTES DELICIOUS WARM OR COLD.
IT PAIRS VERY WELL WITH EITHER PINOT GRIGIO OR SANGIOVESE.

1-2 pound salmon fillet

1 lemon

Salt

Mask:

1 cup sour cream

1 tablespoon **each** parsley and
minced chives **or** green onion tops

1 teaspoon dill weed

½ teaspoon curry powder

1 teaspoon soy sauce

Makes enough to cover a 2-pound
fillet.

Preheat oven to 375°. Remove all salmon bones. Place salmon, skin side down, on a baking pan lined with aluminum foil.

Combine sour cream, parsley, chives, or green onion tops, dill, curry powder, and soy sauce. Completely cover the salmon with this "mask."

Place salmon in oven and cook for 25 minutes. Let stand 5 minutes before cutting.

Serves 4 to 6

Succulent Smoked Salmon

USE EITHER A SMOKER OR A BARBECUE TO PREPARE SALMON.

APPLE, PEAR, OR APRICOT LIMBS ARE GOOD FOR SMOKING OR BUY

FRUIT WOOD CHIPS AT A HARDWARE STORE.

3-4 pounds salmon fillet

2 tablespoons brown sugar

1 tablespoon salt

1 tablespoon cracked pepper

Smoked Salmon Omelet Filling

For a gourmet breakfast dish, fill an omelet with smoked salmon.

  1 tablespoon butter

  4 green onions, sliced
    or 1 small red
    onion, diced

  ½ cup smoked
    salmon, flaked

  ½ package (3 ounces)
    cream cheese

Melt butter and add onions, cooking 2 minutes. Add salmon and cream cheese and heat through.

Serves 2

Dry fish with paper towels. With pliers, pull bones from the center of the fish. Remove side bones with a sharp knife.

Mix together sugar, salt, and pepper. Rub over top of salmon, using more of the mixture on the thicker parts of the fish. Place salmon in a rimmed pan (juices will drip) and refrigerate overnight.

Prepare grill, using the smallest amount of charcoal or heat possible. Use indirect method of cooking by placing salmon on center of grill and charcoal on the sides. An oven thermometer placed on grilling rack should measure about 200°. From the beginning, periodically place fruit wood chips on coals to produce smoke. Cover and cook salmon over very low heat, about 2 hours.

Present salmon fillet whole as an appetizer for a large party or cut into smaller pieces for a first course. Serve with cream cheese or fresh goat cheese, thinly sliced red onions, and sliced baguettes or rye crackers. Smoked salmon keeps up to 1 week in the refrigerator, or it can be frozen.

Serves 8 to 10

Fish in Ginger-Wine Sauce

WONDERFUL AROMAS WAFT THROUGH THE KITCHEN AS FRESH FISH
STEAMS ON A BED OF SPICY AROMATIC VEGETABLES. SERVE WITH
STEAMED RICE, GREEN VEGETABLES, SUCH AS BOK CHOY OR SUGAR PEAS,
AND OPEN A BOTTLE OF PINOT GRIGIO OR OTHER WHITE WINE.

4 ounces fresh ginger root, peeled

2 whole green onions

1 carrot, peeled

3 cloves garlic

2-3 pounds white fish fillet, such as halibut **or** sea bass, cut 1-inch thick

½ cup Pinot Grigio **or** other white wine **or** water

½ cup (one bunch) cilantro, chopped

Soy sauce (optional)

Slice ginger crosswise very thinly. Sprinkle slices evenly on bottom of a large sauté pan.

Cut green onions and carrot crosswise into 3-inch-long pieces, then slice them lengthwise into thin strips. Distribute onions and carrots evenly over ginger. Crush, peel, and thinly slice garlic. Sprinkle over vegetables.

Place fish fillets, skin side up, on top of vegetables. Pour wine over fish. Cover pan, turn on heat, and bring to a rapid boil. Cook 4 minutes on one side, then turn fish over. Top with cilantro, cover pan, and cook for an additional 3 minutes. Turn off heat and let sit, covered, for 5 minutes.

Lift fish from its skin onto a plate; surround with vegetables and sauce.

Serves 6 to 8

MEATS & GAME

Barbecuing is a Western art form, and beef is a favorite choice for tossing on the grill. We've included several grilled recipes, among them Peppered Rib Eye Steak with a Sangiovese Sauce. We also offer Hot & Spicy Grilled Pork Ribs and a Grilled Lamb Roast with Dried Fruit. But if grilling is not your style, you'll find other mouth-watering choices, like Pork Tenderloin & Chive Sauce, Veal Shanks, an old-fashioned Venison Stew, and an exotic Buffalo Bruschetta.

Fire Pit Beef

THIS CROWD-PLEASER TAKES TWO PEOPLE TO PRODUCE MAXIMUM
CULINARY FLAIR. SERVE WITH MASHED POTATOES, SAUTÉED MUSHROOMS,
YOUR FAVORITE SALAD OR VEGETABLE DISH, AND A BOTTLE OF SANGIOVESE.

5-6 pound whole top round **or** chateaubriand

2 cans (4 ounces each) dry mustard powder

1 cup water, approximately

1 bag (5 pounds) rock salt

10 pound bag of briquettes, charcoal **or** mesquite

Preparing the Fire

Use a barbecue with a 12- to 15-inch flat space for coals. Or dig a wide flat hole and line it with aluminum foil. Add charcoal, light, and let burn until no flames show and briquettes are covered with a gray ash. Arrange briquettes to make a flat surface 6 inches wider than all sides of meat. Note that the mustard-and-salt-covered meat is placed directly on the coals. No grill is used.

Take meat out of the refrigerator 1 hour before cooking. Trim fat and dry beef with a paper towel. Place on a platter larger than the meat.

Add water to mustard until the consistency of cake frosting. With a flat knife or spatula, frost the top and sides of meat until exposed surfaces are evenly coated about A-inch thick. Coat with enough rock salt to completely cover the mustard. Then turn the meat over and cover the bottom of the meat with mustard and rock salt. Brush off any excess rock salt. The rock salt and the mustard form a "crust" to insulate the meat.

Prepare barbecue fire (See box at left).

With a helper holding the platter at the side of the barbecue, and with great ceremony, use strong tongs to place meat directly on coals. You can place additional coals around the sides.

Barbecue about 25 to 35 minutes. Then, again with great ceremony, lift meat from coals with tongs. Your helper can break up any fallen crust and rearrange coals to look fresh. Turn meat over and reposition on coals. Cook another 20 to 25 minutes.

Lift meat from coals, brush off coals and burned crust, and place on a platter under a foil tent for 15 to 20 minutes before moving to a carving board and cutting into thin slices. Pour any juices over meat.

Serves 12

Grilled Beef with Wine Marinade

MARINATED IN A RED WINE SAUCE AT LEAST TWO DAYS IN ADVANCE,

THIS BEEF DISH IS DELIGHTFUL GRILLED OR BROILED.

4 pounds beef top round, cut 2 inches thick

½ cup Worcestershire sauce

½ can jellied cranberry sauce

¼ cup soy sauce

½ cup Sangiovese **or** other red wine

Skewers for grilling

Cut meat into 2-inch cubes. Place meat into a heavy-duty plastic bag with a zip-lock fastener.

Whisk together Worcestershire sauce and cranberry sauce. Add soy sauce and wine. Mix well and pour over meat. Seal bag, then turn it so marinade covers meat completely. In case bag leaks, place it in a bowl. Refrigerate at least 2 days. Turn meat occasionally.

When ready to serve, prepare grill or broiler. Remove meat from marinade. Thread 3 or 4 pieces of meat on a skewer. Grill or broil to desired doneness, basting with marinade, if necessary.

Serves 6 to 8

Peppered Rib Eye Steak

FOR A HEARTY MEAL, SERVE THIS STEAK WITH SANGIOVESE
REDUCTION SAUCE (SEE BOX BELOW), GRILLED OR STEAMED
VEGETABLES, AND GARLIC MASHED POTATOES (PAGE 45).

1 teaspoon sea salt **or** Kosher salt

3 cloves garlic, minced

1 tablespoon olive oil

4 rib eye steaks, about 4 pounds

¼ cup black, green, pink, and white peppercorns **or** ¼ cup black and white peppercorns

Using a sharp knife or food processor, mince garlic and sea salt into a paste. Add olive oil. Rub both sides of steak with mixture.

Coarsely grind peppercorns or crush with mortar and pestle. Mix peppers together and spread out on a plate or wax paper. Roll steak in the cracked pepper, packing as much pepper as possible on the meat.

Grill or broil about 4 minutes per side for medium rare. Transfer to a platter.

Serves 4

Sangiovese is an excellent choice to enjoy with the dinner. Rib eye steak also goes by the name of market or club steak. Mixed peppercorns can be found in the spice section of a gourmet grocery store.

Sangiovese Reduction Sauce

2-3 shallots, minced

2 tablespoons butter

1 cup thinly sliced mushrooms (optional)

1 cup Sangiovese

1 cup beef stock

2 tablespoons cornstarch **or** potato starch

In a saucepan over low heat, sauté shallots and mushrooms in butter until soft. Add wine, turn up heat, and reduce sauce by half. Add any steak juices. Combine beef broth with cornstarch and stir into the sauce. Bring to a boil. Cook until sauce is clear, about 1 minute. Serve in a bowl to spoon over steaks.

Serves 4

Simple Skirt Steak

FLAVORFUL SKIRT STEAK WORKS WELL WITH TRADITIONAL
MEDITERRANEAN FLAVORS AND PERFECTLY MATCHES THAT SPECIAL
SANGIOVESE OR NEBBIOLO YOU WANT TO SHOW YOUR FRIENDS.
IF YOU DON'T SEE THIS STEAK IN THE MARKET,
ASK YOUR BUTCHER TO ORDER IT.

1½-2 pounds skirt steak

2 bunches fresh thyme **or** rosemary

2 cloves garlic

Salt and pepper

Trim excess fat from skirt steak and cut into serving-size pieces.

Separate thyme leaves from large stems. In a food processor, or with a sharp knife, mince thyme and garlic together. Sprinkle mixture over top of meat. Lay a piece of plastic wrap or wax paper on top of meat. Firmly pound meat with a flat-surfaced mallet to hold thyme in place. Remove wrap. Dust meat with salt and pepper. Turn meat over, sprinkle with thyme-garlic mixture and repeat the process.

Grill meat over very hot coals, turning as needed, until cooked to your liking. Cut to test. Medium-rare should take about 6 minutes. Serve hot from the grill.

Serves 6

Stuffed Beef Fillets

THE ITALIAN NAME FOR THIS STUFFED MEAT DISH IS BRACIOLE.

SERVE IT OVER A BED OF RIGATONI PASTA AND GARNISH WITH FRESH

BASIL LEAVES AND FRESHLY GRATED PARMIGIANO-REGGIANO CHEESE.

BRACIOLE PAIRS WELL WITH SANGIOVESE.

Stuffing and Meat:

½ pound hot **or** mild Italian sausage, casings removed and browned

½ pound Prosciutto, chopped

½ cup **each** grated Parmigiano-Reggiano and Romano cheeses

¼ cup seasoned Italian bread crumbs

2 cloves garlic, chopped

1 tablespoon **each** chopped fresh parsley, basil, and oregano

1 teaspoon cracked pepper

2 pounds top round, sliced into thin fillets (about 8 pieces)

¼ cup olive oil

Kitchen string

Preparing the Meat:

Mix all stuffing ingredients together. Place equal amounts of the mixture on each fillet. Roll up fillet starting with narrow end and tie into bundles with string.

Heat olive oil in a large sauté pan. Add fillets and brown all sides. Remove meat from pan and set meat aside, leaving oil in pan.

Braciole takes time to prepare, but it can be made in advance and is sure to be a guest favorite. Ask your butcher to slice the meat thin and pound the slices to tenderize and flatten them.

Prosciutto means "ham" in Italian. The best of this salted, dried ham comes from the Parma region of Italy, where it dries slowly for a minimum of 10 months, giving it a succulent flavor. You can find prosciutto in Italian delis and specialty markets.

Marinara Sauce:

1 cup chopped yellow onion

¼ cup chopped garlic

2 cups sliced mushrooms

½ cup chopped fresh basil

¼ cup chopped fresh oregano **or**
   1 tablespoon dry

2 bay leaves

1 teaspoon cracked black pepper

2 tablespoons brown sugar

1 cup Sangiovese

1 can (28 ounces) diced tomatoes

1 can (28 ounces) crushed tomatoes

Cooking the Stuffed Fillets:

Add onion to oil in sauté pan and cook over medium heat until caramelized, about 10 minutes. Add garlic, mushrooms, basil, oregano, bay leaves, pepper, sugar, and Sangiovese. Stir to pick up browned bits and simmer 2 minutes.

In a large pot, heat diced and crushed tomatoes to simmer. Add onion mixture to tomatoes and stir to mix. Add meat, cover, and simmer 1½ hours. Remove cover during last 30 minutes of cooking to reduce sauce. If desired, continue cooking for further sauce reduction after meat has been removed. Skim off excess fat.

Place meat bundles in an oven-proof casserole dish. Remove strings. Pour sauce over bundles and keep warm in a 200° oven or cool and refrigerate up to 2 days. Reheat, covered, in a 350° oven until bubbly, about 40 minutes.

Serves 8

Paul's Pot Roast

WHAT CAN BE BETTER THAN FIXING A FAVORITE FAMILY RECIPE
FOR GUESTS? THIS ONE GAINS TOUCHES OF ELEGANCE WHEN
STEEPED IN ONION SOUP AND WINE.

3- to 4-pound round **or** chuck roast

¼ cup flour

2 tablespoons olive oil

2 cans (10 ounces each) condensed
French Onion Soup

1 cup Barbera **or** Sangiovese wine

3 cans (14 ounces each) pearl onions

6 small white potatoes

1 pound peeled baby carrots **or** 6-7
carrots, thickly sliced

1 teaspoon cracked pepper

Salt to taste

Roll meat in flour. In a Dutch oven, brown meat on all sides in olive oil on medium heat. Add soup and wine, cover, and simmer for about 3½ hours. Turn meat over once during cooking.

Add onions, potatoes, carrots, and seasonings; cover and simmer for another hour.

Serves 6

Smoky Brisket Roast

LIQUID SMOKE IS THE SECRET INGREDIENT IN THIS EASY ENTRÉE OR
PARTY BUFFET DISH. IT'S PURE COMFORT FOOD WHEN SERVED WITH
MASHED POTATOES, YOUR FAVORITE GREEN VEGETABLE, A GREEN SALAD
TOSSED WITH FRESH ORANGE SEGMENTS, AND A GLASS OF BARBERA.

5-6 pounds center-cut lean beef brisket

2 teaspoons liquid smoke

Salt to taste

6 medium-size onions, thinly sliced and separated into rings

1 bottle (12 ounces) **or** 1 cup tomato-based chili sauce

1 tablespoon celery **and** fennel seed

2 tablespoon mustard seed

1 teaspoon black pepper

Rub liquid smoke over brisket and sprinkle with salt. Roast in a 500° preheated oven, turning once, until lightly browned on both sides, about 30 minutes.

In a large roasting pan or Dutch oven, layer half the onions on the bottom. Drizzle half the chili sauce, celery, fennel, and mustard seeds, and pepper over onions. Set meat and juices atop onion layer and place remaining onions, chili sauce, celery, fennel, mustard seeds, and pepper on top of meat. Cover with a close-fitting lid or heavy aluminum foil.

Bake in a 300° oven 4½ hours or until meat is tender when pierced. Open cover carefully to avoid hot steam. Add water or wine if pan becomes dry.

Let cool 15 minutes before slicing meat across the grain. Serve meat and onions together.

Serves 8 to 10

For a make-ahead meal, prepare brisket a day in advance, refrigerate it in onions and juices up to 2 days. Slice meat thinly when cold. Layer with onions in a rectangular oven-proof dish and bake in a 350° oven for 35 minutes, or until meat is heated through.

Brisket makes great sandwiches. Shred meat and heat with onions in microwave. Serve on toasted hamburger buns.

Wrapped in plastic wrap, this recipe freezes well for about 2 weeks.

Hot & Spicy Grilled Ribs

SERVE THESE NICELY FLAVORED SPARERIBS WITH BLACK BEANS AND
A COLORFUL SALAD OF ORANGE AND RED ONION SLICES ON A
BED OF LETTUCE (SEE BOX BELOW). THE RIBS' FLAVOR GOES WELL
WITH REFOSCO, BARBERA, OR SANGIOVESE WINES.

3-4 pounds pork spareribs

½ large onion, peeled and quartered

4 cloves garlic

2 fresh **or** canned jalapeño chiles, stemmed and seeded

2 tablespoons ground allspice

2 half-inch rounds fresh ginger, peeled and minced

1 teaspoon **each** ground nutmeg and salt

1 tablespoon olive oil

Trim fat from meat. Make ¼-inch-deep slashes between ribs on both sides of meat.

In a food processor or blender, combine onion, garlic, chiles, allspice, ginger, nutmeg, salt, and oil. Whirl until puréed. Rub purée over surface of ribs and into slashes on both sides.

Cover and let stand while preparing grill, or cover and refrigerate until next day.

Grill ribs by indirect method over medium heat. Turn occasionally. Cook until ribs are well-browned and meat is no longer pink near the bone, about 1 hour. Cut to test.

Serves 4 to 6

Orange & Onion Salad

1 orange
¼ red onion
½ pound spring greens mix *or* **lettuce**

Peel orange and onion and slice thinly crosswise. Add to spring mix greens or butter lettuce.

Dress lightly with your favorite vinaigrette dressing.

Serves 4 to 6

Grilled Lamb Roast with Dried Fruit

THIS MEAT AND FRUIT COMBINATION PAIRS WONDERFULLY WITH
SANGIOVESE OR BARBERA. CHECK THE RESOURCE GUIDE (PAGE 110)
FOR SOURCES OF ORGANIC, NON-SULPHURED DRIED FRUIT.

1 package (8 ounces) non-sulphured mixed dried fruit, pitted and cut into pieces

½ cup onion, chopped

1 teaspoon grated lemon peel

1 tablespoon chopped fresh rosemary **or** 1 teaspoon dry rosemary

⅔ cup Sangiovese **or** Barbera wine

3- to 4-pound boned and tied lamb shoulder

2 cloves garlic, minced **or** pressed

Salt and pepper

Kitchen string

In a saucepan, combine fruit, onion, lemon peel, rosemary, and wine. Cook, covered, until liquid is absorbed, about 8 minutes. Let cool.

Untie lamb and lay out flat. Rub inside with garlic; sprinkle with salt and pepper. Spread with the fruit mixture. Roll the roast and tie securely at 2-inch intervals. Tuck in ends of roast and tie roll in several places.

Prepare outdoor barbecue for roasting: check instructions for grill. Place meat directly above drip pan. Cover barbecue and adjust dampers to maintain even heat. Cook until an instant heat thermometer registers 130° in the thickest part, 1½ to 2 hours. Remove from heat and let stand 5 minutes before cutting.

Slice lamb thickly, and remove cut strings.

Serves 6 to 8

Pork Tenderloin & Chive Sauce

THIS RECIPE IS EASY TO INCREASE FOR LARGER GATHERINGS.
SIMPLY USE THE SAME PROPORTION OF SEASONINGS TO MEAT. SERVE PORK
HOT WITH GARLIC MASHED POTATOES (PAGE 45) AND CHIVE SAUCE.

Pork Tenderloin:

1 pork tenderloin, about 10 ounces

1 large clove garlic, finely minced **or** pressed

½ teaspoon salt

1 tablespoon anise seed

Chive Sauce:

1 tablespoon butter

1 tablespoon minced shallots **or** green onions

2 tablespoons flour

1 cup chicken broth **or** ¼ cup Pinot Grigio and ¾ cup broth

½ cup minced chives, fresh **or** frozen

¼ cup half and half

Preparing Pork:

Rub pork tenderloin evenly with garlic and salt. Roll in anise seed to cover. Wrap in plastic and refrigerate at least 24 hours.

To cook, preheat oven to 450°. Place pork on aluminum foil-lined cookie sheet and roast for 15 to 20 minutes. Let rest 5 minutes before slicing.

Serves 2 to 3

Creating Chive Sauce:

Over medium-low heat, melt butter in a saucepan. Add shallots and cook until soft and golden, about 3 minutes. Remove from heat. Blend in flour and slowly whisk in broth. Return to heat, simmer, uncovered, stirring occasionally until thick, about 5 minutes.

Add chives and half and half; heat through. Drizzle over pork slices before serving.

Makes about 2 cups

Twice-cooked Pork

THE FIRST COOKING ADDS A SPICY FLAVOR; THE SECOND COOKING
IMPARTS A CRISPY TEXTURE. SERVE THIS MEAT WITH RICE AND
BEANS (SEE BOX BELOW), STEAMED YELLOW SUMMER SQUASH, AND
SLICED GARDEN-RIPE TOMATOES GARNISHED WITH FRESH CILANTRO.
DON'T FORGET A FRUITY SANGIOVESE.

4-5 pounds pork shoulder roast, blade in

1 onion, peeled and quartered

4 canned chipolte chiles

1 bunch cilantro **or** parsley

1 carrot, peeled and quartered

1 tablespoon leaf oregano **and** mustard seed

2 teaspoons cumin seed **or** ½ teaspoon ground cumin

2 bay leaves

Cinnamon stick, 1-inch

6 cups water

1 teaspoon salt

Place all ingredients in a large stock pot and simmer 2 hours, or until meat is tender. Turn off heat. Let meat cool in broth for 1 hour.

Separate meat from broth. Reserve broth and refrigerate. Refrigerate meat up to 3 days.

Preheat oven to 450°. Place pork in a disposable roasting pan and roast until heated through and outside is crispy, about 30 to 40 minutes.

With two forks, pull pieces of meat from bone and place onto a serving dish.

Serves 6 to 8

Black Bean Side Dish

Pork and beans go together, no matter how they are cooked. These two recipes are easy to make—even if a bit exotic.

2 cups dried black beans	Seeds from 2 pods cardamon
1 large onion, chopped	1 can (6 ounce) tomato paste
4 cups pork broth	Salt to taste

Soak beans overnight. Rinse and drain. Combine all ingredients, bring to a boil, and cook until beans are tender, about 40 minutes. Add salt.

Serves 6 to 8

Veal Shanks

A DELICIOUS DISH FOR COOL WEATHER, VEAL SHANKS ARE COMPLEMENTED

WITH A SAFFRON-FLAVORED RICE AND A CRISP SPINACH SALAD.

OPEN A PINOT GRIGIO OR A SANGIOVESE TO ADD TO THE AMBIENCE.

4-5 pounds meaty veal shanks, cut into 2-inch-long pieces

Salt

½ cup all-purpose flour

1 tablespoon **each** butter and olive oil

¾ cup Pinot Grigio

½ cup chicken broth

1 tablespoon grated lemon peel

½ cup fresh parsley, chopped

1 clove garlic, minced or pressed

Sprinkle shanks with salt. Place shanks and flour in a paper or plastic bag. Shake bag to dust flour evenly over meat.

In a large sauté pan or heavy pot, heat butter over medium heat. Brown meat on all sides; remove shanks when browned and set aside. Add wine and broth to pan. Bring to a boil, scraping browned bits from the bottom and sides of pan. Return shanks to pan. Cover and simmer 1½ to 2 hours, or until tender. Transfer shanks to a warm serving platter.

Combine lemon peel, parsley, and garlic into a paste. Bring sauce to a rolling boil, scraping down browned particles. Add paste to sauce. Cook while stirring for 1 minute.

Pour sauce over meat just before serving. This dish can be refrigerated up to 2 days (see box below).

Makes 6 servings

> Meat recipes with sauce can be made 1 or 2 days ahead of serving. Cool, cover, and refrigerate in a non-corrosive container.
>
> To reheat, move to an oven-proof container, cover, and place in a 350° oven for 40 minutes or until hot through. Transfer to a serving dish.

Herbed Veal Chops

BECAUSE THIS FLAVORFUL DISH HAS PLENTY OF SAUCE,
WE SUGGEST SOAKING IT UP WITH A ROTINI OR FUSILLI PASTA.
HERBS AND CHEESE PROVIDE ENOUGH SALT FOR MOST PEOPLE.
THE VEAL DISH PAIRS WELL WITH SANGIOVESE.

1 tablespoon olive oil

Salt and pepper (optional)

4-6 one-inch-thick veal shoulder **or** loin chops

1 onion, chopped

2 cloves garlic, minced

1 teaspoon dry Italian herb seasoning

½ cup red **or** white wine

3 tomatoes, peeled, seeded, and sliced

½ cup chopped Italian parsley

Parmigiano-Reggiano **or** Parmesan cheese, grated (optional)

Heat olive oil in a large sauté pan. Lightly salt and pepper chops. Brown chops over medium high heat. Remove when browned and set aside.

Add onion to pan and cook until soft and translucent, about 3 minutes. Add garlic and herbs and stir together. Cook 1 minute more, then turn off heat. Add wine and stir, scraping bits from bottom of pan.

Return chops to pan and top with tomatoes. Over high heat, bring sauce to a boil, reduce heat, cover, and simmer, turning chops over once, until veal is tender when pierced, 20 to 25 minutes. Remove chops to a platter.

Bring sauce to a boil to reduce liquid, add parsley, and cook for 1 minute more before spooning sauce over chops.

Pass cheese to sprinkle on chops.

Serves 4 to 6

Buffalo Bruschetta

FRUITY SANGIOVESE WINE BRINGS OUT THE SWEETNESS OF THE
BUFFALO MEAT AND BLENDS NICELY WITH THE MEDITERRANEAN
FLAVORS OF THIS OPEN-FACE SANDWICH.

3 frozen sliced buffalo steaks, **or** leftover grilled meat, thinly sliced

1 loaf French/Italian bread (batard)

6 Italian Roma tomatoes, sliced

2 tablespoons olive oil

8 cloves garlic, chopped

1 shallot, diced

4 to 6 ounces mushrooms, sliced

8 to 10 basil leaves, slivered

½ cup **each** grated Parmesan and shredded Mozzarella cheese, mixed

In a sauté or frying pan, heat frozen buffalo patties. Turn sliced steaks after they have browned on one side. Gently break apart sliced steak and continue to cook until completely browned. Set aside.

Slice bread lengthwise and place on a baking sheet. Place tomatoes on bread. Heat olive oil in a sauté or frying pan and sauté garlic, shallot, and mushrooms about 3 minutes. Place mixture evenly over the bread. Place buffalo meat on bread. Top meat with basil and cheese.

Preheat oven to 350°. Place bread in oven until crust is crisp and cheese is melted, about 10 minutes.

Cut into pieces and eat with your hands. Provide plenty of napkins.

Serves 6

Sliced buffalo steak is what the Denver Buffalo Company Resturant uses for a wrapped steak sandwich (burrito).

To grill buffalo tenderloin steaks, use your favorite marinade. In general, buffalo meat is lean and should be cooked at a lower temperature than beef. Check the Resource Guide on page 110 to order a catalog of buffalo meats.

Wild Venison Stew

EVEN IF YOU DON'T HUNT, YOU CAN BUY WILD GAME THROUGH YOUR
MEAT MARKET OR DIRECTLY (SEE RESOURCE GUIDE, PAGE 110). THE SWEET
MEAT OF VENISON PAIRS WONDERFULLY WITH SANGIOVESE AND NEBBIOLO.

2 pounds venison stew meat

1 large onion, sliced

2 cloves garlic, chopped

¼ cup chopped parsley

¼ teaspoon **each** Italian herbs, dill weed, and black pepper

½ cup red **or** white wine

1 beef bouillon cube

4 medium potatoes, diced ¾-inch

2 carrots, sliced ¼-inch

1 turnip, diced ½-inch

½ pound sliced mushrooms

1 tablespoon soy sauce

2 teaspoons Worcestershire sauce

3 tablespoons flour

1 tablespoon cornstarch

2 teaspoons Kitchen Bouquet

Polenta (optional)

In a large sauté pan, heat oil and brown venison and onion. Add garlic, parsley, Italian herbs, dill weed, and black pepper. Stir. Add wine and bouillon cube and 2 cups water. Simmer slowly for 2 hours or until meat is tender. At this point, you can refrigerate meat and continue making the stew the next day.

Place potatoes, carrots, and turnips in a large stock pot and add 2 cups water. Cook about 10 minutes or until potatoes are half-done.

When meat is tender, add to vegetable mixture. Add mushrooms, soy sauce, and Worcestershire sauce. Cook until potatoes are done, adding water if necessary.

Mix together flour and cornstarch. Stir into ¼-cup water. Slowly add mixture to stew, stirring constantly. Cook for 2 minutes or until thick. Add Kitchen Bouquet and serve over polenta, prepared according to package directions.

Serves 8

John Keller built a campsite in Mendocino County 50 years ago where his friends could come during deer-hunting season. Some years they bagged their buck; other years pinochle was the only game around. Whenever they get lucky, John and wife Laura invite the group to their Bay Area home for his celebrated Venison Stew. When you try the recipe, we think you'll understand why these invitations are so coveted.

Hasenpfeffer

THIS RABBIT STEW RECIPE FROM ALASKA WAS ORIGINALLY USED FOR
WILD RABBIT, BUT THIS VERSION WORKS JUST AS WELL WITH RABBIT
FROM YOUR MEAT MARKET. SERVING SUGGESTIONS INCLUDE
WILD RICE PILAF, STEAMED VEGETABLES,
AND A BOTTLE OF SANGIOVESE OR BARBERA.

3 strips bacon

½ cup flour

1 large rabbit, cut into pieces

1 cup Sangiovese **or** Barbera wine

1 jar (10 ounce) currant jelly

1 tablespoon mixed pickling spices

If you prefer, rabbit with sauce can be placed in a casserole, covered, and cooked in a 350° oven for about 1 hour, or until tender. Rabbit can also be cooked ahead, refrigerated up to 2 days, and reheated by placing in a 350° oven for about 40 minutes, or until heated through.

Cut bacon crosswise into ½-inch pieces. In a large sauté pan, cook bacon over medium heat until crisp. Spoon off excess fat. Remove bacon and reserve.

Place flour in a paper or plastic bag, add rabbit, and shake until rabbit is thoroughly covered with flour.

Brown rabbit in bacon drippings. After rabbit is browned, turn off heat and add wine to the pan. Stir to pick up all browned bits. Add jelly, stir to mix, and heat to a boil. Sprinkle pickling spices and reserved bacon around rabbit.

Cover and simmer rabbit over low heat for 1 hour, or until rabbit is tender. Turn rabbit over halfway through cooking. Add more wine or water if rabbit becomes dry.

Serves 4

SWEETS

Today's trend is to skip desserts, but it's nice to have something sweet—especially if you have children. Our choices include something for everyone, from fruit in sauce or on meringue to cookies, pies, cakes, and custard. Most are light and delicate; all are delightful. When combined with a sweet Moscato wine, any selection makes an ideal ending to a meal.

Honey Tangerine & Moscato Sauce

THIS SWEET WINE SAUCE MAKES A PERFECT TOPPING FOR LIGHT DESSERTS.
DRIZZLE OVER MANGOES OR OTHER TROPICAL FRUIT OR ADD TO
FAT-FREE FROZEN YOGHURT WITH STRAWBERRIES.

⅔ cup honey tangerine juice (about 2 large honey tangerines)

½ cup Moscato wine

½ cup refined sugar

2 tablespoons water

Mix tangerine juice and Moscato together in a saucepan over medium-high heat. Bring to a boil and continue stirring until the mixture is reduced by one-half, about 15 minutes. Be careful not to burn sides of pan while reducing. Set aside.

Mix sugar and water together in a saucepan. Stirring constantly, heat on medium-high until mixture is a clear, viscous liquid. Add the tangerine and Moscato mixture to the sugar and water; continue heating, stirring continually, for 30 seconds or until everything is well mixed. Remove sauce from heat and let cool.

Sauce can be stored in a refrigerator up to 3 days.

Makes 1 cup

Fruit Meringue

THIS FANCIFUL DESSERT WAS CREATED FOR ANNA PAVLOVA
WHEN SHE TOURED AUSTRALIA IN 1926. IT IS A PERFECT FOIL FOR
SUMMER FRUITS AND MOSCATO WINES.

Meringue:

4 egg whites, at room temperature

⅛ teaspoon salt

1 cup sugar

1 tablespoon cornstarch

1 teaspoon white wine vinegar

1 teaspoon vanilla

Topping:

1 pint heavy cream, whipped

6 to 8 kiwi, peeled and thinly sliced

Seasonal fresh fruits, such as
  raspberries **or** peaches,
  or frozen fruits

Use a mixer with a wire whisk for beating egg whites. Beat egg whites and salt until frothy. Gradually add sugar, about 1 tablespoon at a time. Blend cornstarch with the last tablespoon of sugar before adding. Beat in vinegar and vanilla. Mixture should hold stiff peaks.

Preheat oven to 400°. Line a cookie pan with cooking paper or lightly grease pan. Pile meringue on paper, shaping it into a high decorative mound about 7 inches in diameter. Place in oven; immediately reduce temperature to 250° and bake for 1½ hours or until lightly browned and dry on the surface. Remove from oven and cool completely. Wrap airtight and store up to 24 hours at room temperature.

Just before serving, swirl whipped cream over meringue. Garnish with sliced kiwi and other fruit. Slice like a cake to serve.

Serves 8

Melted Raspberries

For a colorful red and green dessert, drizzle raspberry topping over the fruit and meringue.

  2 cups fresh raspberries

  2 tablespoons sugar

In a saucepan, lightly crush fresh berries. Add sugar. Heat berries until sugar is melted and berries are juicy. Let cool and spoon over meringue, kiwis, and fruit.

Orange & Almond Cookies

FOR THE BUSY BAKER, THESE COOKIES CAN BE MADE IN ADVANCE
AND BAKED JUST BEFORE SERVING.

1 cup butter, at room temperature

½ cup **each** white and brown sugar, firmly packed

2 eggs

1 teaspoon vanilla

1 tablespoon grated orange rind

2¾ cups flour

½ teaspoon soda

1 cup chopped **or** slivered almonds

Place butter, sugar, eggs, vanilla, orange rind, flour, and soda in a heavy-duty mixer bowl. Mix until all ingredients are blended, about 2 minutes. Add almonds.

To mix by hand, combine butter and sugar. Add eggs, vanilla, and orange rind. Mix together flour, soda, baking powder, and almonds. Stir all together until dough is well blended.

Mold dough into a long smooth roll, about 2½ inches in diameter. Wrap in plastic or wax paper and chill several hours or overnight until stiff.

Preheat oven to 400°. With a sharp knife, cut dough in thin slices, ¼-inch-thick. Place slices a little apart on a greased baking sheet. Bake until lightly browned, about 12 to 15 minutes.

Makes about 50 cookies

Cheese and wine make a classic ending to any meal. Make up a tray of Gorgonzola, Oregon blue, Dry Monterey jack, or various styles of goat cheeses, and pass bread or fruit, such as pears and apples.

For a sweeter finish, choose peach- or orange-flavored cream cheese to spread on whole-wheat biscuits or Orange & Almond Cookies (see above). Always bring cheese to room temperature before serving.

Buttery Lemon Bites

REFRESHINGLY SWEET AND ZESTY, YET WINE-FRIENDLY,

THESE LEMON BITES MAKE A NICE ENDING FOR A MEAL.

CUT PIECES SMALL—INTO A ONE-BITE SIZE—AND

PASS THEM AROUND OFTEN.

Crust:

1 cup butter, softened

½ cup sifted powdered sugar

2 cups all-purpose flour

Topping:

4 eggs

2 cups granulated sugar

1 teaspoon grated lemon peel

6 tablespoons fresh lemon juice

⅓ cup all-purpose flour

1 teaspoon baking powder

Preheat oven to 350°. Cream butter and sugar until light and fluffy. Stir in flour and blend well. Press dough into a 9- by 13-inch rimmed baking pan or dish; bake 20 minutes.

Beat eggs until light and frothy. Gradually add sugar, beating until thick. Add lemon peel, lemon juice, flour, and baking powder. Stir until blended. Pour over hot baked crust, return to oven, and bake for 15 to 25 minutes or until pale golden.

Remove from oven. Let cool in pan. For tiny bites, cut into 1-inch squares.

Makes 48 pieces

Pecan Pie

ALWAYS A FAVORITE FOR THOSE WITH A SWEET TOOTH,

THIS PIE ALSO PAIRS NICELY WITH THE SWEET WINES.

1 9-inch pie shell, homemade **or** commercial

½ cup sugar

¼ cup butter

1 teaspoon vanilla

1 cup white corn syrup

¼ cup milk

3 eggs

1 cup shelled pecans, broken and whole pieces

Bring all ingredients to room temperature. Pre-heat oven to 400°.

To pre-bake pie shell, prick bottom of shell with a fork. Bake for 8 to 10 minutes, until lightly browned. Remove from oven. Reduce oven heat to 350°.

With a spoon or whisk, combine sugar and butter. Add vanilla, corn syrup, milk, and eggs. Stir gently to mix; do not beat. Add pecans.

Pour into pie shell. Bake 50 to 65 minutes until custard is set.

Cool and serve. Refrigerate leftovers.

Serves 6

Always refrigerate eggs or products with eggs in them. To bring eggs up to room temperature for baking or whipping, simply crack the required number of eggs or egg whites into a metal bowl and set the bowl in warm water for 5 to 10 minutes. Use eggs immediately in your recipe.

Sour Cream Apple Pie

MAKE YOUR FAVORITE CRUST OR BUY A CRUST FOR

THIS EASY TO MAKE PIE .

Filling:

¾ cup sugar

2 tablespoons flour

1 cup sour cream

1 egg

1 teaspoon vanilla

¼ teaspoon nutmeg

2 large apples, cored, peeled and sliced

1 deep dish (9-inch) pie crust, unbaked

Topping:

⅓ cup sugar

⅓ cup flour

1 teaspoon cinnamon

¼ cup butter, cut into small pieces

Preheat oven to 400°. Stir sugar and flour together. Add sour cream, egg, vanilla, and nutmeg. Mix well. Stir in apples. Pour into pie shell. Bake 15 minutes, then reduce oven heat to 350° and bake an additional 30 minutes. Remove pie from oven.

For topping, turn oven heat back to 400° F. Mix together sugar, flour, and cinnamon. Stir in butter. Sprinkle mixture over pie. Bake pie an additional 10 minutes.

Serve warm or cold. Refrigerate leftovers.

Serves 6

Apples that hold their shape when cooked, such as Fuji, Braeburn, or Golden Delicious, are best for Sour Cream Apple Pie.

Experiment with the taste of white, red, or sweet wine with dessert. Everyone experiences taste a little differently, so it's bound to be an entertaining evening.

Elegant Cheesecake

THIS CREAMY CHEESECAKE USES ONLY EGG WHITES.

SERVE ALONE OR WITH SLICED FRUIT, SUCH AS

RIPE PEACHES, FRESH CHERRIES, OR BERRIES.

ANY DESSERT WINE WILL MAKE A DELIGHTFUL ADDITION.

Crumb Layer:

1 cup (1 package) zwieback, crushed

1 tablespoon sugar

¼ teaspoon cinnamon

3 tablespoons butter

Cake Layer:

4 egg whites, room temperature

1 cup sugar

3 packages (8 ounces each) cream cheese, softened

½ teaspoon salt

1 tablespoon vanilla

Topping Layer:

2 cups (1 pint) commercial sour cream

2 tablespoons sugar

In a food processor, whirl zwieback into crumbs. Add sugar, cinnamon, and butter. Mix thoroughly. Press into the bottom of an 8- or 9-inch spring-form pan in an even layer.

Preheat oven to 350°. Beat egg whites until they form soft peaks, then gradually beat in the sugar to make a meringue. Cream cheese, salt, and vanilla together until soft and creamy. Fold egg white mixture into the cheese until well blended. Spoon batter into pan.

Bake about 30 minutes. Remove from oven; increase oven temperature to 450°.

Combine sour cream and sugar; spread over top of cake. Return to oven for 4 to 5 minutes until cream is set. Remove from oven and cool until cold. Remove sides from pan, cover, and refrigerate up to 3 days.

Serves 12

Moscato Cake

A LIGHT—AND EASY-TO-MAKE—CAKE THAT DRAWS
RAVE REVIEWS WHEN PAIRED WITH FRESH FRUITS
AND MOSCATO OR MALVASIA WINES.

1 teaspoon vegetable oil

2 tablespoons flour

1 package yellow cake mix

½ teaspoon ground ginger

3 eggs

1¼ cups Moscato wine **or** other white
   wine

*We tried a sweet Malvasia
Bianca with this delicate
cake. Everyone agreed it
was delicious.*

Preheat oven to 350°. Prepare a Bundt or tube pan by thoroughly oiling the interior and dusting with flour.

Mix together ginger and cake mix. Add eggs and wine. Using a beater on low speed, beat for 2 minutes; if mixing by hand, stir for 3 minutes.

Pour batter into pan; bake 30 to 35 minutes. Test by inserting a toothpick into the center. If no uncooked batter clings to the pick, the cake is done.

Remove from oven and let sit 10 minutes. Turn pan upside down on a cake plate and shake gently to remove cake. Let cool before slicing. Keep covered to keep fresh.

Serves 12

Caramel Custard

CUSTARD WITH A CARAMEL SAUCE IS SOMETIMES LISTED
ON A MENU AS FLAN. REGARDLESS OF NAME, THIS DESSERT
PROVIDES A FLAVORFUL FINISH TO A MEAL.

½ cup sugar

3 eggs **or** 6 egg yolks

⅓ cup sugar

¼ teaspoon salt

1 teaspoon vanilla

2 cups whole milk

*Flan and cheesecake are
baked custards, which use
eggs and heat to solidify
their ingredients.
Zabaglione and Crème
Anglaise are examples of
frothy stirred custards.*

In a small pan, melt sugar carefully over low heat until caramelized (brown), about 5 to 8 minutes. Pour evenly into custard cups. Swirl each cup as you pour so that caramel will coat sides. Cool.

With a whisk or spoon, stir eggs, sugar, salt, and vanilla slightly to mix.

Preheat oven to 350°. Heat milk until steaming. Slowly at first, pour milk into egg mixture, stirring constantly. Pour mixture through a strainer into cups. Set cups in a deep-sided pan. Pour hot, almost boiling, water in the pan about 1 inch up on cups. Carefully place in oven.

Bake 30 to 35 minutes, until a knife thrust into the custard comes out clean. Immediately remove from heat and water. Cool and refrigerate.

To serve, turn cups upside down on rimmed dishes. When unmolded, melted caramel runs down sides forming a sauce.

Serves 6

Party Planning

The recipes in this book were developed especially to go with American-grown Italian wine varietals. In our testing, we included white wines, reds, and red blends, from a light and fruity style to a concentrated and bold flavor.

Our findings? All of the wines tested received high marks although individual taste preferences differed. However, any party featuring a good bottle of Sangiovese, Barbera, red blends, Pinot Grigio, Moscato, Arneis, Tocai Friulano, and rosatos with these recipes will be successful.

DINNER PARTIES

At dinner parties, showing many wines, start with a white or a rosato wine. Bring the red wines out for the main course, progressing from light to more intense flavors. Some guests may enjoy white wines throughout the meal. A small glass of Moscato or Malvasia might accompany dessert.

Fill wine glasses only half-full to allow room to swirl the wine and release the fragrance. Use a separate glass for each wine served and allow 1 pour per wine plus a little extra.

For barbecues, potlucks, and casual entertaining, you may wish to pour the same vintage throughout the meal.

PARTY TIPS

Invite guests to arrive no more than an hour before you plan to serve dinner. Pour either a white or a rosato wine and pass 1 or 2 appetizers.

When guests are invited to be seated for dinner, make sure they know whether they should leave their wine glass or bring it to the table.

One bottle (750 ml) of wine equals 24 ounces or 6 pours. One pour (4 ounces) fills a standard stemmed glass one-half to two-thirds full. For a 3 hour reception, plan to serve 6 pours per person. Plan 2 pours with pre-dinner appetizers.

White wine should be chilled 1 hour before serving. Serve whites cool, but not ice cold. Red wines should be served at room temperature, 68° to 74°.

To open a wine bottle, cut the capsule (seal) one-half inch down from the top of the bottle and remove the upper part to expose the cork. Leave the rest of the seal on the bottle; it's part of the design. Some bottles are closed with plastic corks to protect flavors.

Remove the cork when you're ready to use the wine. Wine "breathes" in the glass, not in the bottle. If you're opening an older wine (over 20 years), remove the cork just before you plan to drink it; older wines are fragile and tend to lose their bouquet shortly after being poured.

Selecting & Cellaring Wine

Touring wineries is certainly the most romantic way to buy wine. You have a chance to see the vineyards and learn a little about the winemaking process.

Once you select your wine, where will you store it? Whether you plan a cellar for your wine library or make space for a few bottles, we offer some storage tips.

STORING WINE

From wine cellar to closet, no matter where you stash your bottles, here are a few guidelines.

Wine should be stored in a cool, dark, quiet place at a constant temperature (50°-60°) to keep it from aging too rapidly and losing its finesse. Sunlight and fluorescent bulbs also affect flavors.

Keep wine away from motors that produce vibrations. Bottles need to be secured and above water level if you live in an area prone to natural disasters such as earthquakes or floods.

Wine can be stored in its original case. Just be sure that the wine in the bottle is in contact with the cork. A controlled humidity of 58% keeps corks from drying out.

For maximum quality, let wine rest at least a week after traveling before you open it.

BUYING WINE

There are two ways to buy wine—direct from the winery or from a wine merchant at a local shop, supermarket, or discount store. Each option has advantages.

On a trip through wine-producing regions, you'll have a chance to sample different vintages and varieties of American-grown Italian varietal wines in winery tasting rooms. Though you pay retail prices for wine, buying it here assures correct storage prior to sale.

If you encounter hot weather on your wine tour, don't leave bottles in your car. Wines warmed above 90° tend to degrade. Be sure to carry wine in the air-conditioned part of your car, not in the trunk.

Though you may not be able to taste the wines you buy at a wine shop, you will usually get expert help in finding a wine to match your meal and budget. You may also uncover some great bargains through closeouts or special sales.

Supermarkets and discount stores may have the lowest prices but no assurance of professional assistance. Our suggestion: buy a bottle and take it home to try; if you like it, buy a case. Remember, great bargains sell quickly.

INDEX

Resource Guide—Wine-Friendly Food Series

Publishing wine-friendly food cookbooks involves delightful research and surprising discoveries. Testing each recipe, then savoring several American producers' Italian varietal wines with the dishes, are experiences I wish I could share with you. Unfortunately, I am not able to invite you into my kitchen or to join me on winery visitations. But this is an exciting time to learn about wine and food. For example, I often learn about an additional winery bringing a new Sangiovese or Pinot Grigio wine to market.

To keep information current, I am using several innovative ways to let you, the reader, share in my discoveries. These communication methods range from the Toyon Hill Press web site, to a fax-by-request service, to the reliable postal service.

The fax-by-request service, **1-650-851-5579**, presents a variety of up-to-date faxes regarding wine-friendly foods, sources for unique ingredients, and American-grown Italian varietal wineries. You call from a fax machine and select pages for delivery back to your fax machine. This service is free, costing you only a phone call.

I have developed a list of the wineries producing American-grown Italian varietals. I present my discoveries of new and unusual recipe ingredients, cooking methods, and personal opinions about wine-friendly foods. I catalog sources for unique food products, spices, and cooking tools that you can order shipped to your door. Also I give suggestions where to find ingredients. Try the fax-by-request service, for some delightful discoveries.

You can visit my Toyon Hill Press web site at **www.toyonhillpress.com.** Current information, similar to that available through the fax-by-request service, is posted. There are recipes, unique to the web site, as well. Through the web site, graphic information, like pictures and maps, is available to you. Links to many other wine, cooking, winery, and travel sites are presented for your investigation.

Your opinions, thoughts, and innovative suggestions are important to me. Comments from you will help me plan future publications. Specifically, I welcome your contributions regarding matching American-grown Italian wines with a variety of dishes. I am also interested in your thoughts about the wines produced by American wineries. Your comments may appear on the web pages or in the fax-by-request service offerings (**1-650-851-5579**) unless you tell me otherwise.

To share your joys, comments, and queries about Companions at Table, here are two more ways you can contact me: e-mail me at **margaretsmith@toyonhillpress.com** or write to me at **Toyon Hill Press, 118 Hillside Drive, Woodside, CA 94062-3521**.

Margaret A. Smith, Publisher

Toyon Hill Press

WINE-FRIENDLY FOOD SERIES COOKBOOKS

Companions at Table, Food to Serve with American-Grown Italian Varietals by Margaret Acton Smith and Barbara J. Braasch. Recipes from wine lovers to match with Sangiovese, Barbera, Moscato, Pinot Grigio, Arneis, and more.

Rhône Appétit, Food to Serve with American Rhône Varietals by Jane O'Riordan. An experienced chef, Rhône wine producer, and daily homemaker presents her recipes for Rhône wine-friendly foods.

Zinfandel Cookbook, Food to Go with California's Heritage Wine by Janeth Johnson Nix and Margaret Acton Smith. Over 100 home kitchen-tested recipes from Appetizers to Desserts to serve with Zinfandel wine.

☎ Toll-free telephone orders: **1-800-600-9086**

Have your MasterCard or VISA ready.

⌨ E-mail orders: **margaretsmith@toyonhillpress.com**

💻 Visit our website at **www.toyonhillpress.com**.

✉ Postal orders: **Toyon Hill Press, 118 Hillside Drive, Woodside, CA 94062-3521, USA**

📄 Fax orders: **1-650-851-5579**

☾ Office Telephone: **1-650-851-9086**

I wish to order the following books:

____ **COMPANIONS AT TABLE** Paperback, first edition $17.95 Calif. sales tax $1.49

____ **RHÔNE APPÉTIT** Paperback, first edition $17.95 Calif. sales tax $1.49

____ **ZINFANDEL COOKBOOK** Paperback, first edition $14.95 Calif. sales tax $1.23

Sales tax: California residents please add sales tax.
Shipping: $4.00 for the first book and $2.00 for each additional book.

____ Check

____ MasterCard or ____ VISA Card number _____

Name on card _____ Exp.date: month ____ year ____

Name: _____

Address: _____

City: _____ State:____ Zip: _____

Telephone (____) _____

Also available FREE: *Toyon Clippings* newsletter _____ Place my name on your mailing list.

CALL TOLL-FREE AND ORDER NOW

I understand that I may return any books for a full refund, for any reason, no questions asked.